TWICE RESCUED

A NEW VIEW OF LIFE
FROM THE BOTTOM OF THE CLIFF

Gene McMath

WORD & SPIRIT PRESS

Twice Rescued: A New View of Life from the Bottom of the Cliff

Author website: http://www.GeneMcMath.com

Published by Word & Spirit Press
Tulsa, Oklahoma   USA
http://WandSP.com
e-mail: WordandSpiritPress@gmail.com

Printed in the United States of America

ISBN 10: 0-9785352-3-5
ISBN 13: 978-0-9785352-3-0

Cover design / Interior design and page composition by Bob Bubnis / BookSetters, Bowling Green, KY

Scripture quotations labeled NIV are from the HOLY BIBLE, NEW INTERNATIONAL VERSION. Copyright © 1973, 1978, 1984, International Bible Society. Used by permission of Zondervan Bible Publishers.

Scripture quotations labeled NLT are from the Holy Bible. *New Living Translation* copyright © 1996, 2004 by Tyndale Charitable Trust. Used by permission of Tyndale House Publishers.

Scripture quotations labeled *The Message*® are copyright © 1993, 1994, 1995, 1996, 2000, 2001, 2002 by Eugene H. Peterson. Published by NavPress. Used by permission.

Dedication

To my older brother Norm, who was always, and still is, looking out for me. I love you, bro!

To my sister Donna and her husband Wes, who supported me in every one of my endeavors. Thanks for proofing!

To my two oldest brothers, Weldon and Eldon, from whom I have learned more than anyone will ever know. May you finish strong!

But mostly to Mom and Dad, who not only gave me the ability, but also the responsibility, to think for myself. After all these many years, you are still the best parents ever, and I love you with all my heart!

And to my daughters, Stina and Selah, who see the real me. I pray that your journey is as rewarding as mine, without the heartache!

Finally, to my beautiful wife, Cindie, who, after 25 years of marriage, is the gal I have always dreamed of wanting. Thank you for sticking with me through all the stuff!

This is for you!

ACKNOWLEDGMENTS

Thanks to John for believing in me and telling me that this story needs to be told.
Thanks to Mark and Bob for seeing this book through to its completion.
Thanks to all of my friends along the way who have been a part of the journey.
And, finally, a special thanks to Cindie's family.
I can not say enough to repay your love.

Contents

Preface

Remember in the Bible where God tells us something like, ". . . I know the plans I have for you. They are for your good and not for bad." (Paraphrase mine)

Well, sometimes I just want to throw up my hands and say, "What is that all about?" If God has such a good plan for me why do I go through all this crap? (Yes, that is the word I used. I know the King James translators have the Apostle Paul use the word "dung," but I think my word is more fitting for today.) I don't know, maybe the *dung* that I deal with is my own fault, but the good and bad along the way has created an incredible adventure. It seems that the ups and downs all come together in the end to equal the positive.

Some people are very good at making life choices and setting goals to determine where they will be in five, ten, or even twenty years. That is *not* me. I have always simply taken the road that presented itself (or even left the road for a more unplanned adventure!). I would never have dreamt of finding myself where I am today. It just happened to me, as you will read most things in my life have happened. My habit of not planning ahead has driven some of my friends crazy. It may have even driven me crazy from time to time, but for some reason, that is just who I am.

Now that I have stopped long enough to gaze out on the beauty of this incredible adventure, I am happy to say that I can now see good unfolding where I once thought I only saw crap! In fact I would have to say, "God *really does* cause everything to work together for good..." (Romans 8:28).

So the following, as the old bumper sticker more or less reads, *"Just Happens!"* I invite you to *examine* this unbelievable journey that will take you to heights of adventure, and depths of failure only to find God waiting in both places. I pray that the pages ahead will help you comprehend God's "plan for good" where you see only bad in your own life. The adventure before you may be indescribable, but then again, so is God.

Enjoy the journey.

CHAPTER ONE

Climb

I was raised in a Christian home and have always attended church. When I was a small child, I heard the pastor say to our congregation that we should kneel and pray until we heard from God. I knelt down at a back pew and said, "God, if you are real, show me a sign." As I knelt, I looked up through an old six-pane window to see two small clouds in an otherwise empty and beautiful blue New Mexico sky. One cloud was white, the other, black. The two clouds passed each other, becoming one for a short time, then separating again. With my child-like mind, I took that as God's message that He was real and would come again to take those who believed in Him back to heaven.

From that point on my story is typical of a young person who drifted back and forth from acceptance to rebellion, until as a teen one night, while sitting in a bath-tub trying to wash the smell of cigarette smoke from my body, I decided that I had had enough.

My older brother told on me! After I confessed, I learned that he didn't even really know that I had been smoking but was just being mean, as older brothers usu-ally are. At any rate, I sat in the tub and told God that I was too old to receive a whipping from my mother for doing nothing more than smoking. I told Him that either I was going to have to get my act together or He was going to have to change my mother's heart! "And by the way Jesus," I added, "could you please punish my brother for getting me into this mess?"

For some reason, though, the only person God cared about that night was the one sitting in the tub smelling of smoke. I didn't choose being caught in this situation! It just seemed to choose me! I had played my hand, and now there I sat, face to face with God, knowing that it was time to make a decision. It was then that I felt a call to serve the Lord full-time. I didn't have a clue what that meant, but serving Him part-time was sure not working out so well. So, I decided to give it a shot.

My father had bought me a damaged, department store guitar, for only $5.00. But when I first saw it, I was excited. I began teaching myself how to play, practicing after school several hours a day. Eventually, I became fairly good at playing it. I wrote songs and dreamed of travel-ing all over the country singing in churches and concerts. I thought that maybe someday I would even record an album to proclaim the reality of Christ's love. I would stand in front of the mirror and imagine the announcer proclaiming to the expectant crowd, "Ladies and gentlemen, Gene McMath!" The crowd would erupt in cheers and applause, I imagined, and I would play for them, which I really did, all the while looking into the living room mirror. I would become famous!

After graduating from high school, I moved to Albuquerque, New Mexico, to play with a Christian rock band. I soon fell in love with a girl whose parents were diplomats in Central America and had her in the United States to attend school. We dated for less than a year, but for some reason, when her parents discovered our relationship, it was all over. I just figured that as soon as they found out that she was dating a nobody like me, they ordered her home! She called me on a Wednesday night with the news, and I put her on the plane Thursday afternoon, sure that I would never see her again. I was crushed. Everywhere I looked reminded me of her, and I found myself walking around in a fog. I was heartbroken—at eighteen. I do not recommend this for young people. It is far better to put off such pain until later in life. To make matters even worse, the band I was playing in wasn't very good! So I took my broken heart and drove back to the small town I was raised in to visit my parents for the weekend.

On the drive back to Albuquerque, I quite accidentally met my brother at an intersection in the middle of nowhere. He was returning from a Colorado town where he had just accepted a position as a church pastor. He suggested that I move there to help him with the church. With the way things were going in Albuquerque, I thought, *Why not?* Within a couple of months, I was living in the beautiful mountain town of Gunnison, Colorado.

I became the youth leader in the church, which of course offered to pay me. Feeling honored and wanting to wear this new role with humility, I refused the money and said that I would donate my time. (Now that was stupid!) So I got a "real job," being a paperboy. At first I delivered the papers to dorm students on campus. Then I added a driving route on the north side of town. The Lord blessed my efforts (or so I thought), and before long I owned the whole distributorship.

I would get up at 2:00 a.m. and drive my truck empty over the Continental Divide, then swap it for another truck full of newspapers, auto parts, and other cargo. I would drive back to Gunnison and deliver products to stores and papers to paperboys. This routine started a cycle: the more I worked, the more money I made; and the more money I made, the more I worked! Before I knew it, I was working eighteen hours a day, six days a week, and nine hours on the seventh! (That was my Sabbath.) Maybe I wasn't working that much for an ambitious, single guy in his early twenties, but one thing is for sure: I had stopped playing music.

When I had first arrived in Gunnison, the newspaper ran an article on me and called me "an accomplished guitar player." Since that was the first time anyone had said that about me, I was surprised. I mentioned it to my brother, who agreed, "Of course, you are an accomplished guitar player." But now, just a few years later, my talent, my gift, my dream, and my calling were all sitting in the corner collecting dust with my guitar!

It's not that I had stopped serving God. I was still very active in the church, although as I recall I was no longer the youth leader. But I fell in love with one of the youth in the church. I decided not to let this one get away, so when my brother moved on, I stayed put. Later, when she grew up to the ripe old age of eighteen, I asked Cindie Sebring to marry me.

Her father was on the board of directors for Middle East Gospel Outreach, and as a result, he, Cindie, and I, along with Cindie's grandmother, went on a tour of the Middle East with Elias Malki. With Cindie's father's permission, I purchased a ring in Bethlehem near the birth place of Christ and presented it to her that night at the hotel in Jerusalem. Lucky for me, she said, "Yes!"

From Jerusalem we went to Cairo, Egypt, for more than a week. Near the end of the tour, we rented a van and driver to take us across the Suez Canal, deep into the Sinai Desert, so we could climb Mt. Sinai. The day of our trip, we left Cairo at 6:00 a.m. After crossing the Canal, we traveled all day across the desert, in and out of spectacular mountains, and then right up next to the Red Sea, only to repeat the whole process over and over again for hours. Finally, at sun-down we reached the base of Mt. Sinai.

At the base of the mountain is a small airport with a restaurant. After sweating and complaining all day, having to rough it in an air-conditioned van, I thought surely I had glimpsed how the children of Israel must have felt. We could have flown, but instead we wanted to catch the *real* experience. Now that we had finally arrived, the restaurant seemed so inviting that we ate a nice meal of rice and potatoes (no manna!) before going to our rented rooms next to the airport. We sat outside a few minutes, gazing at the brilliant starry sky, and then went to bed around 8:00 p.m., only to rise at 1:00 a.m. Shortly there-after, we started climbing the mountain in order to reach the top by sun-up. It was of course pitch black as we hiked up the side of the mountain, with only flashlights to show the path in front of us. Just as the Israelites traveled thousands of years earlier, trusting only in God's fire by night and cloud by day to lead them, there was nothing to see except the next step in front of us. It was important always to stay in the light in order not to step right off the side of some unseen cliff.

I reached the summit just as the sun peeked over countless mountains scattered across the Sinai Peninsula. It was truly one of the best memories in my life. I found it interesting that, as we reached the top, not only were there a Swedish gal and a French man sharing a sleeping

Gene on top of Mt. Sinai just after sunrise

bag, where they had obviously spent the night, but there was also a small church of some sort that had been built right on top of the mountain. I thought the secular intermingled with the religious on such a historically spiritual location was quite an interesting sight.

After an hour or so at the top of Sinai, we headed down what seemed to me to be the east face of the mountain. Although, now that I think about it, my directions

Looking off Mt. Sinai onto St. Catherine's Monastery

were so messed up that I was convinced the sun rose in the west that morning. We had climbed around from what I thought to be the south side, which was gradual and fairly easy. Now we were dropping quickly, straight down on stairs made of rocks carved out of the mountain side. It was very rugged and dangerous if you lost your step, but if the pilgrim kept his eye on the narrow path and stepped carefully in the places that had been marked out it was not overly difficult.

Taking this path down, at the bottom of the mountain one finds St. Catherine's Monastery, which was constructed by order of the Emperor Justinian between 527 and 565. It is built over the top of what is said to be the sight of the burning bush that Moses encountered in order to start this whole journey. Inside the monastery there are over 3,500 volumes of ancient writings in many different ancient languages. There are also many other Christian relics to see. All in all, it would take many more hours than the few minutes we had allowed after a long night of hiking. It is truly a place filled with historic wonder. After spending some time in the monastery, we hiked back to the airport for lunch and to load up for the journey back to Cairo.

After lunch, just before we loaded into the van, I noticed activity on the tarmac. A military band and small group of soldiers marched into formation, standing at attention, as if something important was about to happen. Soon a helicopter settled in next to them. A distinguished Egyptian got out wearing a crisp western suit. I continued standing at the door, fascinated by the scene but not knowing what was happening. To my surprise, the suited man walked right up to my door, stopped and looked right at me, as though I should do something. I'm sure I looked every bit the naïve twenty-one-year-old American I was and very out of place. After studying me a moment, he shrugged and walked through the doorway.

The excitement was over, so I left the doorway and got into the van. "What was going on there, and who was that man?" I asked the driver as we took off.

"Oh, that was Hosni Mubarak, the vice president of Egypt."

Eight days after we returned from Egypt, President Anwar Sadat was assassinated, and Mubarak became president. I had stood just feet from him, without having a clue of where I really was or whose presence I was in.

We all returned safely to the United States, and Cindie and I announced our engagement. We married soon after, on August 14, 1982. Our home church had sold the church building in order to build a new one, so we were married in The Community Church in Gunnison. Cindie's dad had bought her a car which I sold to my best man on our wedding day. As a result, no one knew what car we were going to leave the wedding in. It was a secret that I held closely. Cindie did not even know which vehicle to get into in order to escape the two hundred or so people who attended our wedding. But as I watched her walk down the isle toward me, I realized that I could no longer keep any secrets from her. As we knelt to pray during the ceremony after saying our vows in front of the audience, I whispered into her ear. "We will leave in my Suburban."

After the wedding, we found that some friends who did not know what was going on had jacked Cindie's car up and put blocks under the tires so we couldn't leave. To their surprise, we walked right past her car, got into an old beat-up Suburban, and drove off. Except for one of my groomsman's jumping into the front seat and forcing Cindie to sit in the back, it was a perfect get away.

After spending two weeks in Australia touring the Gold Coast for our honeymoon, we returned to find the new church building being constructed in Gunnison. I went back to work, returning to my same routine, with one exception. When I would get off, after working most of the night I would go out to the job site and help the new pastor pound a few nails.

I remember sitting on top of a three-story scaffold, holding a circular saw upside down while exposing the blade so that I could cut off the truss endings. The saw was heavy, and after cutting a few trusses, I set the saw down . . . on my leg and sliced it to the bone! Now I had even shed blood for Jesus. *"I am truly a great Christian,"* I thought to myself, *"sacrificing life and limb for Christ and the church."* I even ruined a good pair of overalls, blue jeans, and my brand new pair of long-johns. Still it didn't bother me much, but for some reason my brother-in-law and the pastor both became a little queasy. I don't think the open wound bothered them as much as the foot-long needle that the doctor kept sticking into it. When the needle went in, they went out of the room. The doctor said the shot would stop the pain. I tried to tell him that the needle hurt much worse than the saw blade did. But you know doctors; they always think they know best! So now not only did I have a big opening in my leg, but I had a needle sticking out of it too.

It took several days to recover to the point where I could at least go back to work, but I didn't read the warning in this mishap. I was enjoying a heady combination of being young, working a lot, having fun, making lots of money, and sleeping very little. My mother says I started walking at nine months and hadn't slowed down since.

In everything I did, I would go 100 miles an hour and not know how to stop. I was always on the go, making money and spending it as fast as I could. My father-in-law used to say that I was burning the candle at both ends. I thought that was his way of saying I was very bright. I owned a house on the river, and more automobiles than I could drive. Between Cindie and me, we owned 5 automobiles, of which at least three sat in our driveway at a time. I always had cash on hand to do pretty much whatever I wanted to do. But all that stopped in little more than the blink of an eye. Our quick descent from Mt. Sinai less than a year before seemed only to foreshadow the plunge that was about to take place and start the roller coaster ride of a life time.

CHAPTER TWO

Fall

On the first of June, I shoveled snow off my front lawn . . . that had been there since October! In the winter, vacationers fly into Gunnison to snow-ski at Crested Butte, but in the summer, they drive RVs in by the droves to camp out. It is often said that there are two seasons in Gunnison; "Nine months of winter, and three months of company!" The winters are long and hard, only to be separated by incredibly beautiful summers.

The scenery is gorgeous, with water in abundance! There are scores of lakes and rivers in the area that vacationers enjoy all summer. In fact the north-south streets in town have ditches next to them flowing with river water. The city diverts the water from one river on the north end of town to make it flow down the streets to another river on the south end of town. Residents use pumps to siphon the water out of the ditches as it passes in front of their homes to water their lawns.

Locals live in Gunnison mostly to enjoy a life full of outdoor excitement. Hunting, fishing, skiing, and rafting are all a way of life. The *unofficial* motto at the college is "Ski Western State, and get a diploma in your spare time."

This was my mindset when Cindie and I married. Even though I did not snow-ski or enjoy the winters that much and having to drive over a mountain pass every night made one grow weary of winter in Gunnison, I loved the summers. Life was full of excitement, and when I was not working, I was hard at play!

I had purchased a home on the Gunnison River north of town. Cindie was raised at the east end of town on the same river. Even before we were married, we spent many summer afternoons getting in the river on inner tubes at my house and floating down stream for an hour or so, getting out at her house. It was a very relaxing and exciting way to spend a beautiful sunny summer afternoon in Gunnison.

The water is mostly cool and clear as you float down the river. But occasionally you run across some rapids as the river cascades over rocks at a faster pace. It is these peaceful times of simply floating and enjoying the scenery, interrupted by the sheer madness of managing the white water, that make river rafting—and in our case inner tubing—so enjoyable.

One time before Cindie and I were married, we decided to take the church youth group, along with some adults, on a rafting trip. Instead of getting in at my house, we decided to go another few miles up stream and get in at Cindie's grandparents' place. This would make for a much more exciting adventure, since there was such a large group of us.

We had a whole pickup-load of inner tubes and one large raft that we put in the water that day. My brother, Cindie's father, and a few other people were in the raft. We had never floated this part of the river before, but it seemed to be very peaceful. That is until we rounded that one bend.

Suddenly the river took a sharp turn and became very swift. Several people, along with my brother's elementary-school-aged son, all of whom were on inner tubes, were ripped from their tubes by the current. Having seen this, my brother stood up in the raft to see where his son went, and at that point their raft capsized as well. All on board suddenly found themselves in the water.

Cindie's father, who cannot swim and was not wearing a life vest, found himself being pushed along head over heals under the water only to pop up from time to time just long enough to catch his breath and go back under. He told me later that, as he was in the water, he remembered seeing on television that people always drown with their eyes open.

So he said, "I just closed my eyes."

Sure enough he floated right to the top and stood up under his own power in complete control.

After a few moments of utter terror, everybody regained their composure and found their way to shore. After recapturing the raft and the inner tubes, we finished our trek down the river. Once again, another exciting day on the river and all was well.

Maybe sometimes it would be better to know where you are going before you head out, but then again life does not afford us that opportunity, even though (as I have learned) river rafting does!

One summer, after Cindie and I were married, we had company visiting from California. Their son and daughter had been the ring bearer and flower girl in our wedding. They had come to Colorado several times to visit.

Once, before we were married, we took them river rafting. That trip was very peaceful, with no troubles at all. We floated down the river gently and had a great conversation about marriage and life, as they counseled us on unforeseen troubles that might come along the way. Cindie and I talked with them about how we were going to live our years together enjoying each other right there on the river. All was at peace as we rafted on that day.

Now that we were married and they had returned for another visit, we decided to take them on another rafting trip. As with the earlier trip, this one would be peaceful and full of conversation. But first I would have to get up early in the morning and drive over the Continental Divide to swap trucks in order to collect my load for delivery in Gunnison.

I tried to talk our visiting friend into getting up at 2:00 a.m. to ride with me over the mountain pass. He refused! I guess he was too lazy to get up that early. I joked with him that if I drove over the edge of a cliff that morning, it would be his fault, since he wouldn't be there to keep me awake. Later I apologized for that joke. It turned out to not be so funny.

I have driven over Monarch Pass around 1300 times in my life. It transverses the Continental Divide at 11,312 feet above sea level, between the towns of Gunnison and Salida, which are about sixty-five miles apart.

I can describe every corner in the road. I know where, without warning, mountains jut up and canyons cascade down next to the road. It is a beautiful example of God's creation, intruded upon by man's ingenuity.

Several months earlier, I had had a dream of driving over the Pass in the middle of the night and seeing a man lying in the middle of the road. In my dream, I knew the exact spot on the road where he was lying. I can still see it vividly, over twenty years later. As you can imagine, the dream woke me up, terrified.

Less than a month later, at 4:00 a.m., as I rounded the corner less than one half of a mile from that spot, I really did find a man lying in the middle of the road. My dream had terrified me, but when it actually happened, I was horrified!

I called for help, and an ambulance took him to the hospital. He had been at a party at the ski area and left walking on foot, drunk. Apparently, he was picked up by some guys in a van who became angry with him as they traveled down the road. So they simply opened the door and kicked him out.

Many times I have wondered why I dreamed about that event just before it happened in real life.

I can tell many stories like this from those 1300 trips over Monarch Pass—stories that include everything from spinning out of control on black-ice to flat tires leaving me stranded in the middle of the night twenty miles from the next civilized area.

Once during the winter when I was in white-out conditions at the bottom of the Pass, I dozed off for just a second and simply drove off the edge of the highway at 55 miles an hour. I was on a perfect straight-away, but when I hit the bank of snow left by the plow on the roadside, it sucked me right into the ditch.

During winter the trip over the mountain can be very treacherous. On many trips, white-outs due to blowing snow made it so that I could not see past my windshield. Even in the summer, it can snow at 11,000 feet above sea-level, but not on this August morning. On this day, the forecast was, "clear skies and beautiful sailing ahead!"

I loved driving over the mountain at night in the summer. It was very peaceful and quiet. I would sing to keep myself awake as I drove for hours on the high mountain roads. The views were memorable: snow-covered peaks reflecting the moon's rays, tree lines casting shadows across the valley, large numbers of deer feeding in the moonlight. On occasion, a solitary elk would cross my path, its majestic horns strutting up into the air as he escaped my sudden, blinding appearance on the highway.

There is no place on earth like the Colorado Rockies! Mountains are everywhere. Gunnison rests in a valley at 7,703 feet above sea level. To leave Gunnison, you have to cross through a mountain pass, the highest of which is Monarch.

I don't even remember going to bed that Wednesday night, even though I know I did. The last thing I remember is standing at the bottom of the stairs before going up to my bedroom. The plan was that, when I got home from work, we would eat and then raft the river with our friends.

As I got up that Thursday, August morning, the air was cool and crisp, with the stars shining bright. No snow or moisture of any kind. It was going to be a beautiful day. Sunrise was just four hours away.

I left at 2:00 a.m. alone.

On the west side of the Pass, a little over two miles from the bottom, is a place called "Barrel Springs." It is fairly well known locally, because there is a 35-gallon barrel sitting under a pipe that juts out of a cliff on the right hand side as you travel down the mountain. The pipe carries a constant flow of spring water that spills into the barrel. You can pull over and park to take a drink of this fresh spring water, right out of the pipe, if you wish.

Just across the road is a 300-foot cliff that goes pretty much straight down. The view is spectacular, and if you stop and look, you will notice an old blue car at the bottom of the cliff. Apparently the highway department left it there to give tourists something to talk about as they peer over the edge.

I recall saying on many occasions as I passed by Barrel Springs that I would never want to drive off the road there. The person who runs off the road at that spot would never live to tell about it!

This morning I had already driven over the Continental Divide, exchanged my empty truck for one full of supplies, and begun my return. I had topped the mountain and started down the western slope, working my way around the corners, as I always had, keeping my rig in the same gear that I used to climb the mountain in order to keep my speed in check as I traveled down hill.

No one knows for sure what caused it to happen, but on August 25, 1983, at 4:30 in the morning, just two miles from the bottom of Monarch Pass, my life forever changed! Rounding the corner at Barrel Springs, the brakes locked, and I headed straight toward the water barrel. Then the load in my truck shifted, and it spun 90 degrees to the left and shot straight off the edge.

The highway department had just put up a new guard rail, which I used as a ramp. On the way down the cliff, the truck first hit at 150 feet below the highway. I was not wearing my seat belt, so at that point I must have taken

Black marks of my truck leading over the edge of the cliff

out the windshield with my head. At least that is what happened, according to the policeman. Personally, I know that I am a coward and probably jumped out of the door. At any rate, the truck and I played leap frog over each other the rest of the way down the cliff. Massive rocks of all shapes and sizes tumbled down the cliff at the same time and half-way buried me alive as I landed straddling a boulder! And yes, if you are wondering, that does hurt! The truck, now only a few inches tall, came to a stop just a few

The remains of the truck at the bottom of the cliff

feet below me. It was totally crushed, and if I had still been inside of it, I would have been crushed as well!

The fact that I was no longer in the truck was the good news, but I was still lying there more dead than alive, broken and mangled in the midst of all those boulders. Another trucker climbed over the edge of the cliff to see if anyone was alive. He heard my screams of hysteria and immediately called for an ambulance on his CB radio.

The bad news was that at this point my whole body was nothing more then a blood-soaked shell with a head swollen to the size of a basketball! I was so disfigured that no one could tell who I was! It turned out that the truck driver who found me was renting a trailer house from me at the time, but even he did not recognize me.

From the time they found me, it took three hours to get me back up the cliff and to the hospital in Gunnison.

The doctor, who was a friend, later said that he had never seen a more broken body and did not know why I was still alive. Other then shaving my head and putting 50 stitches in it, there was nothing, or very little, he could do. So he called for a helicopter from St. Mary's Hospital, in Grand Junction, where there was a neurosurgeon. I had always wanted to fly in a helicopter! Now I would have my chance but wouldn't ever remember it!

To make matters even worse, I didn't have my wallet with me, so no one knew for sure who I was. At the time, I was 23. I had been married one year and eleven days. The policeman knew my father-in-law had family in the paper business, so he called him. I am sure it must have been a terrifying phone call for my in-laws to receive, but it turned out to be blessing, because it saved Cindie from receiving the policeman's call. Cindie was able to hear about the wreck from her father. He told her that I had run off the road and my back was hurt. He said, "They have taken him to the hospital to check him out. I'll pick you up and take you there."

Cindie had no idea that more than just my back was hurt. When she arrived at the hospital in Gunnison, she asked the doctor if she could see me. He responded by saying, "Let me clean him up first." After a few minutes, he came back and said that she could now go in to see me. Her reaction was one of shock and denial.

"I walked through the swinging, double doors and saw a person sitting there, half lying down, half sitting up.

He had a large, black head and breathed just like Darth Vader" (from the movie Stars Wars), she later recalled. At that point she looked around, turned, and walked out of the room.

"My husband is not in that room!" she exclaimed as she walked back through the swinging doors.

I recall in the Bible how Jesus had been beaten beyond the point of recognition during the crucifixion. Remember when Mary first saw Jesus in the garden but did not recognize him? Many say that his resurrected body differed from the corpse buried three days earlier, but I can't help but wonder. Was it just too surreal for her to comprehend? Was it not that she didn't recognize him, but rather that what she saw differed so much from what she expected?

Remember when Jesus was walking down the road with some guys who knew him from *before,* and yet they didn't have a clue about who He was? To think that no one recognized Him after taking such a beating, to have given so much and be recognized so little for it, must have been a very sad event indeed. Even Thomas, one of Jesus' own disciples, had to actually stick his earthy hands into Jesus' open wounds before he could recognize Him! It must have been a very painful event—for both parties!

To have witnessed that event would have been so moving. Two people locked into a life-changing moment together by the earth-shaking occasion in which they found themselves.

The helicopter came and flew me to Grand Junction, 120 miles away. Cindie was forced to ride with her mom in their car, since the helicopter was not large enough for a passenger. It was on that trip that Cindie realized what was happening. Losing her composure, she began to cry out that she was too young to become a widow at the age of nineteen. Her mother quickly took charge and said, "Do you think God would have let him live this long just to let him die now?" She encouraged Cindie to pray. Thank God for mothers-in-law!

At the Grand Junction hospital, I was wheeled into the emergency room on a gurney, where the specialist was waiting. He checked me over very carefully. Along with my basketball-sized head, due to a serious closed-head injury, I had many other problems! One of them was the fact that my right lung was collapsed, and I was having trouble breathing. He needed to operate to inflate my lung but was afraid that I would not survive the operation. He could not even give me medication because of the closed-head injury. He said that he was unable to see inside my head because of the swelling and thought that medication might cause more damage. He prepared my family for the worst and suggested that they begin making funeral arrangements.

"If he does live, he will be an invalid for the rest of his life," the doctor told them as he sent me to intensive care. "All I can do is place him in this bed and watch him. If he lives, he lives. If he dies, he dies."

I lived!

In fifteen days I walked out of the hospital a new man. I was told stories of miraculous healing for injuries of which I was unaware. I was told that by the next morning my lung just *seemed* to heal itself. My right cheek bone was crushed, but once the swelling subsided in my head and doctors went back in to repair it, they found that it was no longer even cracked! As I walked up and down the hospital halls, I was told of how my back was broken but now no longer seemed to be a problem.

When I first woke up in the hospital and was able to move, about five or six days after the accident, I was sitting on the edge of a chair. The nurse was having me bend slightly forward to check the range of motion in my lower back. There was a machine in front of me with a chrome strip around it. As I bent forward I noticed some kind of monster in the machine looking back at me. I would rise up slightly and then lower myself to see the monster staring at me from inside the machine. After several times, I stopped and gazed into the chrome on the machine only to have the nurse say, "What are you looking at?"

To which I replied, "I am not sure."

As she bent over to see what I was staring at she responded with, "It's you!"

It was only a scab of a swollen, bruised face with two slits where there were once eye sockets!

It is hard for me to explain, but as the blind man in the Bible whom Jesus healed said, "All I know is once I

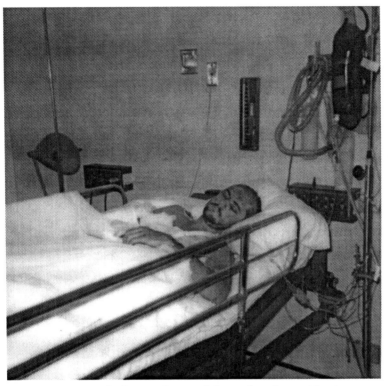

Gene in the hospital several days after the accident

was blind but now I see," I simply say, "All I know is I should be dead, but now I live!" By the time I left the hospital I had gone from the brink of death to the fullness of life in fifteen short days.

But not all was good. The neurosurgeon said that my right side was not working properly. He watched me walk and held his mouth in funny positions. He asked me to walk again and then wrote stuff down. I thought he was making fun of me, but I couldn't read his writing. Honestly, I don't think there was anything wrong with my walking. I had been doing it since I was nine months old. I knew that walking was not my problem. My problem was my arm! It would not work at all.

My right scapula was broken into several pieces. The doctor said that it looked like a mirror that had been dropped and shattered. My right shoulder was mangled and "bent" so that the ball of my arm would not fit into the shoulder socket correctly. The doctor operated, but I was unable to withstand the pain of the post-operation traction; therefore, the operation was unsuccessful. To make matters worse, he said that there was nerve damage and I would not be able to lift my arm over my head, or even high enough to play the guitar. I left the hospital with my arm in a sling, unable to lift it or even move it above the elbow. My guitar playing days were over. My dream had come to an end before it ever started!

After several months of learning how to tie my shoes with one hand, my left one at that, and how to eat left-handed, I became weary. It wasn't that I didn't appreciate my left hand. It proved to be very useful. The problem was that I could not use my right arm. I could not even lie on my belly. I'm not sure if it was because of the position of my shoulder or the fact that I couldn't catch myself as I went face down onto the bed, but for some reason I was unable to lie on my stomach, and I was tired of it. Just try to sleep on your back all the time. After a while, you get tired of it. Besides, I think my snoring was keeping me awake!

One day alone at home, I put a couple of pillows on the couch to make for a soft landing. I'm not sure why, but I didn't even move the coffee table. Maybe I wasn't strong enough to move it, but at any rate I jumped face first over the coffee table onto the couch. My right side was facing the back of the couch, and of course when I hit, my right shoulder hit first. I heard a pop and felt the shot go through my body. *Now I've done it,* I thought as I lay there on my stomach. *When Cindie comes home she is going to be so mad! How will she get me off this couch? Nothing to do now but sleep and pray for the best.* My arm didn't even hurt! In fact it felt kind of good.

A few weeks later we went to Carlsbad, New Mexico, to visit my brother, who was now the pastor of a church there. It was late spring and the temperature was around 104 degrees. I was in the swimming pool when someone suddenly threw a beach ball over my head. I instinctively reached up and grabbed it, not thinking a thing about it, with my right hand! I stood there in the water holding my hand over my head and began to cry. No, it did not hurt; I was healed!

As soon as I returned home, I grabbed my guitar and began to write. One of the first songs I wrote was "Songs to You."

> *I lift my voice to praise you*
> *I sing my songs to you*
> *I lift my hands to worship*
> *Your name so pure and true*

As the flower bows its head in the rain
And the sun comes and shines on it again
It raises its petals as if to sing
And to the King it brings

I lift my voice to praise you
I sing my songs to you
I lift my hands to worship
Your name so pure and true

We all need the rain
We have to feel the pain
So when the sun shines again
To the King we can sing

I lift my voice to praise you
I sing my songs to you
I lift my hands to worship
Your name so pure and true

Today I play the guitar almost every day. I raise my hands above my head daily. When I was in high school, I was quarterback of the highest- scoring football team in the state, but now that God has healed me, I can throw a ball harder than at any time in my life! God totally healed me.

I am not an invalid! I walk, talk, and think as normally as I ever did, although some would say that is not a great feat! I never did act that "normal." Therefore, I am at a great advantage! If I make a bad move while playing cards, I just blame it on brain damage. At least now I have an excuse for acting dumb!

When I walked out of the hospital only fifteen days after the accident, there sat the helicopter that had flown me there. I walked over to it and placed my hand on it, looked up at the warm sunshine and took a deep breath. Never had life been more precious. When one stares death in the face and then walks away from it, life takes on a whole new meaning. I had had dreams and goals, things I was someday going to do. Suddenly I realized that someday may never come. I knew that we have no promise of tomorrow, yet God had given me a second chance. I was not going to miss this one! "Someday" was here!

CHAPTER THREE

Adventure

While growing up in New Mexico, I had written several songs. Now that God had given me a second chance at life, I immediately set out to record them. I was put in touch with a studio owner in Santa Fe who was looking for people just like me to record. I contacted him and allowed him to hear some of my music. Before I knew it, I was living my dream of recording an album entitled "Living by Faith," produced by Tommy Walker. At that time Tommy was a long-haired nineteen-year-old kid who worked at a local fast-food place and lived with the owner of the studio. It all seemed so easy! Santa Fe was a short drive from Gunnison. I also had a sister living in Santa Fe, so recording there was easy. It was obvious to me that God was putting it together.

After finishing the recording, Tommy suggested that I go to Europe to work with Karen Lafferty in Amsterdam for the summer. He had spent a summer or two there and said that it was the best time of his life. So naturally, without any thought, I contacted her. I found that she was in charge of a Youth With A Mission program called Musicians for Missions. I applied and was accepted into the Summer of Service missions program.

Once again, before I knew it, I found myself living my dream. God was obviously on the move, and I was hanging on for the ride of my life. I knew all along that God was going to take me to incredible heights, and I had my eyes set on the highest of heights. I could envision every step that was going to take place before it happened, and God seemed to be right in step. He was taking me from one level to the next.

But the ride was not without some heartache. We arrived in Amsterdam only to learn that we were going to live in an old boarding house for sailors just down from Central Station. Our room was only nine feet wide by nine feet long. There was hardly room for the door to open with our bed (consisting of two bunks pushed together) taking up most of the floor space. Holland is about one-fifth the geographic size of Colorado, with 14,000,000 residences, most of them in Amsterdam. Colorado, on the other hand, has only around 3,000,000 residences! Moving into this small room in the middle of a very large city was not an easy thing for this small-town boy to do. I remember the first words out of my mouth, as I entered the room: "Oh Cindie, I am so sorry." To

Cindie and I in Amsterdam

which she immediately replied, "For what? This is going to be great!" She is a trouper, for sure!

I began playing with a band that performed in the city squares. People from ever facet of life were listening to our music. One time I looked out on the crowd to see a black woman in her early twenties wearing basically nothing but chains and carrying a knife. She was cursing,

45

spitting, and threatening the crowd. Her goal was to stop them from hearing our message. I have to admit that I was a bit frightened by the scene, only to look up again a moment later to see Cindie standing face to face with the lady, holding her hand and praying. I am sure the lady did not accept Christ, but all her powers and actions became stifled as Jesus confronted her that day through my wife. Needless to say, everyone in the band was in awe of Cindie's courage!

Another time we played across town late one night only to realize that we had missed the last tram back to Central Station. All the trams went to Central Station in order to connect with city-buses that would take us to where we lived. I immediately found a city map and charted out the shortest path back to our room on foot. By then it was in the very early morning hours. What I did not know was that my short-cut was going to take us right through the Red Light District.

The Red Light District in Amsterdam is like no other Red Light District in the world! Women stand in windows as gentlemen walk by and *window shop*. If a man likes what he sees, he simply goes into the door next to the window, and the lady closes the curtains while they do their *business*. After the transaction is complete, the man leaves the *shop*, and the gal opens the curtain to attract more business.

All of that of course is the *pretty* side of the picture. As bad as that sounds, the ugly side of the picture is the fact that many of these gals are trapped in their situations by drugs and even slavery. Some of them have been offered jobs and a way out of poverty in some foreign country, only to find that the way out of their earlier situation was nothing more than a snare into drug addiction and prostitution.

Many of them, some of whom we visited with personally, hated men and were diehard lesbians who agreed to be with men only for the pay! It is sad to see tourists go there and gawk while taking pictures of these women, as though the Red Light District were a tourist attraction.

As we walked through there that night, we found ourselves watching our step to avoid stepping on human feces. The streets were dark, trash strewn across the pavement. Policeman sat behind caged-in-windshields, protected from the violence outside in their armored vehicles in dark alleys. It was a lonely and sad sight to behold in the middle of the night, but we arrived at our room around 2:00 a.m. safely. God had allowed us to view the horrors of sin at its deepest level.

Walking through those streets reminded me of Sodom and Gomorrah, when the angels came to warn Lot of destruction, only to have the men of the town ask Lot to send them outside so they could have sex with them.

That summer in Amsterdam was not all dark and gloomy though. While there, we were scheduled to spend a week in De Bron, Holland, at the Christian Music Festival, where Christian artists from all over Europe and the United States would gather.

One day I went to the cafeteria to eat dinner. As the place began to fill up, I saved a seat for Cindie. For some reason she never came, so I had a friend save my two seats and went to find her. When I found her, she was in the room sitting on the bed. I asked her what was wrong and why she did not come to dinner. Her response was, "I just feel like God wants me to fast and pray this meal." *Pretty radical,* I thought to myself, but she has a black-and-white view of spiritual things, so I simply said, "Okay," and went back to the cafeteria.

Back at the cafeteria, I found every seat taken, except the two I had saved. As I took my seat, I noticed one other man walking around, looking hopelessly for a place to sit. He too, I found out later, was without his wife and felt very out of place. I told him that my wife was not coming and invited him to sit down in her chair. He was very thankful, and we immediately struck up a conversation. That man, Peter Goetz, turned out to be the National Director of Youth for Christ in Denmark.

I told him my story, and he told me his. He said that he was there looking for an American musician to come to Denmark to perform. Needless to say, I was excited and offered to let him listen to the tape I had recorded with Tommy Walker. After he heard my music, he asked me to come to Denmark and hold concerts in the public schools for two years! I accepted, and Cindie and I relocated to Denmark for the school years of 1986-88. That event changed my life in every way.

As my dad says about his experience serving the United States during WWII, "I would not take a million dollars for that experience and would not do it over again for a million dollars!" so also was my time in Europe— the most difficult and yet the most rewarding experience I have ever had in my life.

If Cindie had not been obedient to what she felt God wanted her to do during that meal, I probably never would have met Peter, and my life would have been completely different. I am who I am today because of that "happen-chance" meeting and the subsequent two years. Sometimes the little things that seem insignificant to some may be huge eternally!

Because of that event, for the next two years I performed to thousands of students in different schools every day in Denmark and across Northern Europe. I had a concert in the morning and then went into the classrooms in the afternoons. While I was touring in Europe, a record company offered to record another album of my new music. As a result, I recorded my second album, "Life is Calling." Top musicians from all over Scandinavia were in the studio recording my music, songs that I had written. It was happening so fast that I was living my dream and didn't even realize it. Now I was on a mission, and things were falling into place. I just knew that this was the album that would take me to the "big time" in the United States. I began to see the final goal. God had taken me from the lowest of lows to the highest of highs.

Promotional picture

Upon release, the album gained great reviews and was even put on the front page of a Danish Christian newspaper as the most-promoted album for the company. As a result, a television station in Copenhagen contacted me and asked if they could make a 30-minute special entitled simply, "Gene McMath." The producer of the album and I had dinner with the television producer a couple of times to discuss the program. Then we went into the television studio and recorded the special. I performed several of my songs from the album (actually I lip-synced them, but don't tell anybody) and was also interviewed about my testimony. Later that month, the special was aired all over Denmark. I remember riding on a train one day and looking over to see the man across from me reading a newspaper. As I looked closely, I realized that my name was on the back of the paper in a section that contained the TV guide. There it read, "Special with Gene McMath, at 8:00 p.m." Needless to say, I was very impressed with myself! But I'm not so sure God was. He was taking me for a ride, and all the while I thought I was taking Him.

My conservative, Pentecostal upbringing taught me that I knew the correct and only way to salvation. We had all the answers, and it was our job to convince sinners of them. We were told to witness all the time, but the witnessing we had been taught was a monologue type of interaction. The only evangelism ever modeled was done from the church pulpit. Therefore, witnessing was an "in your face" event. Our message was more important than the people we were trying to reach. We did not need to listen to the person we evangelized. He was lost; we were found. He was blind; we could see. We thought that we had all the answers, while in reality, we didn't even understand most of the questions.

We believed that since Christians had all the answers, we should be on the offense. We even quoted Scripture to prove it! It was our job to go into the highways and byways and compel them to come in. Lives were in the balance, and it was our responsibility to rescue them. Witnessing became offensive! And plenty of people were offended! Evangelism meant "insult someone in the name of Jesus!" We were not drawing people to God, but rather pushing them away. No wonder statistics tell us that while approximately 90% of Americans say they believe in God, fewer than 50% go to church. They are not rejecting God, they are rejecting us! God never told us to shove Him down people's throat, but that is exactly what many of us are trying to do, all the while calling it evangelism. As a result of our poor delivery, people lose out on meeting and knowing God personally. This message is too important to cause someone to reject just because we do not know how to deliver it!

I am sure that these criticisms challenge some of us who "have tasted the goodness of God." But it is true: for those who have never recognized God's goodness, this type of evangelism is rude. Imagine how well this type of evangelism would have gone over in a European public school. If I had presented Christ in that manner in a school in Denmark, it would have been the last time I, or anybody from Youth for Christ Denmark, would have been able to introduce Christ to the students at that school. I knew enough to know that I had to learn a new way to present Jesus. Without question that lesson is the most important, and I believe the most profound, lesson I learned while in Denmark.

Those two years in Denmark taught me a new idea that actually is nothing new at all. I learned that the person is more important than what I have to say. That means caring and conversing with the individual, whether he accepts Christ or not. Therefore, *evangelism is simply getting the person to ask the right questions.* Our responsibility is to present ourselves in a way that spurs those questions. This is exactly what I began to do in Europe.

In the concerts, I would tell stories that would generate questions in the minds of the young people. As a result, when I went into the classrooms, I was asked some very good questions by the students. Some of these questions were deeply spiritual. It was in Denmark, in the classroom, that I learned the meaning of true evangelism. In a public school setting, I was openly discussing Christianity with students, and it was absolutely fine! The students were starting the conversation. I was just answering their questions.

One time I was in a tech school when the question arose about creation. I was asked how I believed the world began. There was one young man who said evolution was a fact and there was no God. I did not attempt to argue with him or even show him my point of view. Instead I began to speak about peace and love. What I said really astounded him. He thought my beliefs on peace and love were great and wished everyone believed that way. This same young man ended up coming to the night concerts. He eventually asked me how he could become a Christian.

On another occasion, I was having all kinds of trouble as I backed my car up to the door to unload the sound system. It was a Monday morning, it was raining, and the car was not running properly. *This is going to be one of those days,* I thought as I stepped out into the rain. After the concert, I went into a classroom with about twenty students. About half-way through the class period the question came, "What do you think about the Danish church system?" A dangerous question to ask an American, but I told them what I thought, and surprisingly they all seemed to agree with me.

The church system in Denmark is of course the State Church system. While around 98% of the total population are members, fewer than 2% ever go. The local Danish church is not made up of families as it is here in America. Parents do not see the need to raise their children in such an irrelevant institution. To them the only reason for the church is to provide people with birth, baptism, confirmation, marriage, and death certificates. All other aspects of the church are just for old people who need something to comfort them in their loneliness.

In answering their church question, I was able to talk about the reality of Jesus' love and how He could affect their everyday existence for the better, even when they are young. We discussed matters such as who was responsible for a child's salvation. Interestingly enough, they all seemed to think that it was the parent's responsibility. I assume that this is due to the belief in child baptism.

After a silent pause I asked, "If you were to die tonight and found yourself face to face with Jesus, and He said, 'Why should I let you into my heaven?' What would you say?"

Just then the bell rang and class was over, but no one moved! "Would you like me to tell you the answer?" I asked.

"Yes!" came the response from all over the classroom.

"The answer is, 'You shouldn't,'" I replied with a smile. The class laughed as tension released across the room. And then I continued, "Except..." and right then and there I gave them the plan of salvation.

As it would happen, the school principal had come into the classroom. After I finished speaking, he quickly took control of the class and said, "So you see class, it all boils down to the words in the last song Gene sang in the concert, 'Life is calling you. What will *you* do?'"

As my mind went back to how the day started, I thought to myself, this is definitely *not* one of "those days"! Now even the school principals are witnessing for Jesus!

Everyone is longing to know Jesus! If we will simply learn how to deliver the message, people will want to hear what we have to say. What He has to say! That is what evangelism is all about: presenting Jesus so that others actually *want* to know Him.

At first, these types of events were very exciting and fun. Then as I realized all the souls hanging in the balance, they began to be taxing and hard. In fact it was overwhelming, until God slapped me up side the head and taught me what was really going on.

God taught me that I was just a tool that He was using to reach the lost. No one comes to the Father unless

55

they are called by Him. It is impossible to be saved unless the Spirit draws. I had to come to grips with the fact that I was not responsible for everyone's salvation.

Whoa, what a concept! If we are not responsible for everyone's salvation, then that means we are off the hook! God is the one responsible! God has a great plan for our protection. If we will learn only how to introduce people to Jesus correctly, all the pressure is off! If the people choose not to believe, they are rejecting God, not us. If they believe, He receives all the glory, not us. It is a pretty good trade-off. God gets all the glory and we get none of the blame! Once we realize that, evangelism becomes a breeze!

With this new revelation in mind, I fell into a routine. I created and then performed the same program over and over again. I could do it from memory without even thinking about what I was doing. I knew exactly when the audience was going to laugh and when they were going to cry. I knew exactly when to pause for effect and when not to. I had a story to introduce each song, some of which I had written and some that were simply old folk songs. I even performed "You Are My Sunshine" and had the boys sing it to the girls. I talked about love and how true love was something that could not be earned, followed by singing one of the songs that I had recorded, "Love is for Free." Everything was geared toward planting questions in peoples' minds so that they could ask me them later.

I remembered seeing tears in the eyes of young girls who would say to their teachers that they "wished they could believe like Gene McMath." It was simply the best evangelistic tool I had ever seen in my life. People actually wanted to hear about Jesus on a personal level!

There was only one problem. We had nowhere to send the students after I left. Many times I thought to myself, *I dare not lead this child to Christ. It would be infanticide.* I could easily present Jesus to them. I could easily plant a seed. I could easily give them a glimpse of what it could be like if only they accepted Christ. But to pray with them and then tell them that "Now you are Christian!" would have been like giving birth to a new-born only to leave it out on the street to die! In many cases there simply was no church to do the follow up!

In Europe there are two types of churches: Free Churches and State Churches. Many of the people who go to the Free Churches, which of course are protestant evangelical churches, believe that they are the only true Christians in Europe. To me, the Free Church Christians seem to be simply American Christian transplants. They talk like American Christians, believe like American Christians, and get most of their doctrinal reasoning from protestant evangelical American Christians. They are very critical of the State Church and, spiritually speaking, stand back and throw rocks at it. Many times, they see the State Church as the enemy! For that reason, their own fellow countrymen do not comprehend Free Church Christians. As a result, the Free Church Christians have very little effect on the culture. Their own culture sees them as strange, and, unfortunately, some of the Free Church Christians see that as a positive.

On the other hand, those who ascribe to the State Church simply have a hard time understanding the Free Church Christians. To State Church Christians, which includes the vast majority of the country, the State Church is a legitimate government agency, even though they rarely if ever attend services. The State Church is something that can be trusted, something that is there to meet the public's spiritual needs. Why anyone would not be part of it, much less attack it, is beyond them. Meanwhile, within the State Church, which of course is full of faults, you can find some very loving and strong followers of Christ.

Yes, it is true that well over 90% of the entire population of any given country in Europe is a member of the State Church, but fewer than 2% ever attend! Yes, it is true that fewer than 1% of the members of the State Church ever pray. Yes, it is true that some pastors or priests in the State churches are not even true followers of Jesus. But it is also true that some priests and parishioners in the State Church are working hard to reach the lost through a system that is accepted and trusted by the population around it. The only problem is that these workers are few and far between.

For all of these reasons mentioned above, I believed that there was simply no one, or very few people, who could actually do the follow-up of new converts! This became a real struggle for me in Europe. I began to ask the question, "Who will disciple?" My spirit slowly began to break as I realized the sad answer to the question. There was simply no one available.

As time went on, I began to wonder if we don't have the same problem here in the United States! Some of us are so dedicated to *"our cause in Christendom"* that we have become a subculture and have ceased to affect the culture around us positively. The result is that few are taking young converts and teaching them to mature into reproducing Christians. That in turn aids in creating a society that is rejecting the church because they see a lack of real substance.

Those who reject the church actually think that they are rejecting Christ and that He lacks substance for their life. In reality, however, they have never even met Jesus. How can you reject a God whom you do not know? They do not know Him because in many cases we have not presented the true Jesus to them. We should at least give them the chance to honestly reject God. We need to live our life in a way that entices them to know Jesus. Then we need to follow up and educate them on who Jesus really is, as opposed to simply what we think about Him. Without discipleship, new converts are vulnerable.

So leaving new converts behind began to weigh very heavily on my mind in Denmark as I went from one concert to the next. Danish society was hurting. Divorce was causing an increase of families with only one or no parent. Many children, if they lived with a parent at all, found themselves alone many mornings because their parent did not come home the night before. Other times they woke up to a stranger in the house, as their parent brought someone home for the night. As a result, these children did not know the true meaning of love. In many cases, they had never been loved. Or at least they had not experienced the freedom behind pure love. They were unwanted pregnancies resulting in unwanted children who were now looking for love in all the wrong places. Sex was common among these young people, who were willing to try anything to feel loved.

I remember one night at the end of a concert a young lady told me that she was free because she had a new boyfriend every month. She thought that I was not free at all. She was challenging my statements. I responded by saying that I was free because I did not have to have a new lover every month. I was secure in myself and knew that I was loved and did not have to look over my shoulder. I did not have to worry about what someone else thought about me the next day. I was free because I knew that I was loved no matter what. At that she hung her head. I could see the longing in her eyes, but I could not reach into her heart.

We both left sad. She could not grasp the love of God, and there was not enough time for me to convince her of it. All I could do was plant a seed. I was off to another school, never to see her again. To make matters worse, there was nowhere I could send her.

During another concert, I recall seeing one young man who was wearing work boots. It's not that the boots were special, but it must have just been the way he was sitting that made me notice them, notice him. For some reason he stood out because he looked so sad and alone. After the concert, my interpreter mentioned the same young boy. I remember her saying, "Did you notice that boy with those hunting boots? He looked so sad." She had the exact same feelings about him that I did. As we left, he walked out of the room, and I never saw him again. He never spoke to either of us, but we both knew that he was hurting. It is as though God had spoken to both my interpreter and me, and yet neither one of us could reach into his hurting world.

I felt so guilty because he was alone and we did not even have the chance to visit with him. It was as if the Holy Spirit had whispered to me that the spirit inside of him had evaporated. He was alone with nowhere to go. All we could do was pray, which is no little thing, but somehow I still felt helpless.

Looking back, I can now see why Jesus says in Matthew 9:37, "The harvest is great, but the workers are few"; and why, in John 4:37, He says, "You know the saying, 'One plants and another harvests.'" It truly takes more than just an evangelist, or a missionary, or a pastor. It takes all of us! The harvest was ripe, but there was a desperate shortage of workers. All I could see was the misery and desperation of lost students. The burden was almost more than I could bear, and near the end I found myself longing to escape from the front in the spiritual war in which God had placed me.

At the end of the two years, a well-known Christian artist, Don Francisco, asked me to tour with him back in the United States. I thought I knew all along what God was doing. It seemed too obvious. He had rescued me from the accident for this very purpose. Now He was enabling me to reach my full potential! I now had a lot of performing experience and had recorded an album to take home with me. The miracle was continuing, from the bottom of a mountain cliff to the height of stardom. God was showing off His power, and I was the benefactor! *Dreams,* I thought, *really do come true.*

After leaving Denmark, I toured with Don all across the southern part of the United States and was able to share my testimony and perform the title cut from my album, "Life is Calling." I met people I had admired as a youth and was able to enjoy personal conversations with them at the dinner table.

One day we were leading worship for Melody Green at Last Days Ministries, not long after her husband Keith had been killed in a plane accident. After the service a young man walked up to me and said, "Gene McMath, from Mountainair, New Mexico?"

I replied, "Yes."

To which he replied, "I'm John Chitwood."

I could not believe my eyes. John was a kid I had grown up with in New Mexico. I think he heard me sing and play the first song I had ever performed in public with a guitar. And now God had brought me full circle.

I thought I was living the big time, and my friends from back home could see me!

God had moved in my life incredibly starting in 1983, when He rescued me from death and placed me on a journey that took me through two musical recording projects, over two years of touring in Europe, culminating in touring with a renowned Christian recording artist in the United States. I knew that God had His hand on my life and that there were surely great things in my future.

But it all came to a sudden end before reaching my final goal of having a top record deal in the United States. Don decided to stop traveling in order to lead worship in a local church. There was no conflict or other reason, and I supported Don's decision. It was the right thing for him to do, but it ended my dreams. The avenue that I thought God had planned for my success dried up as fast as it had started. We performed our last concert together in the Mabee Center on the campus of Oral Roberts University in Tulsa, Oklahoma. Then it was all over. I was left without a job, income, or avenue to fulfill my dream. I honestly believed God had let me down.

Several months earlier, on my way back to the United States, I had written a song that included the words:

They call him a Christian soldier
but he's wounded deep inside.
They think that he's a hero
but he's crushed and wants to hide.

He comes home from the battle field
and never says a word.
It's the gore of the details
that never will be heard!

Now I knew all too well how true those words appeared to be! My "ministry" was over.

I had spent two years on "the mission field" trying to convince a hurting and longing society that someone actually cared for them. In the end, I was exhausted. The mission field had weighed so heavily on my psyche that I came home broken. I was a missionary casualty, and no one even knew I had been wounded! Then to make matters worse, my dream of being a Christian recording artist in the United States ended, abruptly and suddenly.

Hebrews 12:27 states that *everything that can be shaken will be shaken so that only that which is unshakable will remain* (paraphrase mine). Needless to say, I felt that God had shaken me to the core and the only thing left was my belief in Him. But that too was about to be shaken!

CHAPTER 4

Just west of Colorado Springs a mountain juts approximately 14,115 feet into the air. In the late 1800's, early settlers struggled to cross the plains, praying for their first glimpse of this mountain. Just a few miles west of what is now the eastern border of Colorado lies a little town called First View. On a clear day, from there you can catch, just peaking over the horizon, the first sight of this mountain that we now call Pike's Peak. Once those early settlers saw that peak, they knew their journey was almost complete.

It is a beautiful mountain as far as flatlanders are concerned, but if truth be told, it is only one of fifty-three mountain peaks in Colorado that stretch over 14,000 feet into the air. If the early settlers were going to continue west after reaching Pike's Peak, their journey had really just begun! The mountains west of Pike's Peak truly show God's awesome creative wonder. But outside of Colorado, no mountain is as well known as Pike's Peak.

Viewed from the east, Pike's Peak cuts a distinctive outline. Even if I close my eyes, I can still vividly picture it. Anyone who has seen it as many times as I have can describe how the southern side of the mountain slowly and gradually slopes to a lower flat area before holding steady, even reaching back up as though needing to crest one last time before letting go of its majesty as it slopes toward its base. The north face of the mountain gradually cascades downward until it eventually relaxes into the beautiful foot-hills of the Front Range. All the while, in the center of the picture, the Peak reaches into the sky as if to say, "Lift up your eyes to the hills and see where your help comes from." It is a beautiful sight indeed. But Pike's Peak does not show the same outline from every direction.

If a person who had seen Pike's Peak only from the east tried to describe its majesty to one who had seen it only from the west, the Westerner, who lives in the middle of those other fifty-two *14er's* could argue that the Easterner had no idea what the mountain really looks like! Nothing from the Westerner's view resembles what the person from the east describes. You could even argue that the two individuals might not even be talking about the same mountain.

The fact of the matter is that no mountain looks the same from any two given directions. But it is still the same mountain. Whether you are seeing the mountain from the east or the west, it is still the same mountain. Not to mention those who view it from the north or the south. Or how about those who view it from the northeast? They can see the same mountain too, but the outline is never the same as it is from another viewpoint. There is certainly more than one way to look at a mountain.

This is exactly how I felt after returning from Europe. I had seen the mountain from more than one side, and now I could not comprehend the "single-side-viewers." I had been raised in the church, but now that I had experienced European missions, I was catching a glimpse of another first view.

I saw how the church operated—or didn't operate—in Europe. I saw how Christians in Europe viewed Christianity. And most of them did not view it at all the same way as I had back in the United States. At first this bothered me, and I thought that they surely were wrong in their theological approach. It was as if they were simply attaching their own cultural belief system to their religious outlook. Now suddenly back in the United States, I realized that we Americans were doing the very same thing. I don't know, I guess every culture does. We all have our view of the mountain.

The problem occurs when we think that our view is the only correct view, while we reject everyone else's view as wrong. This seemed to be the problem I found in the American church as I returned from Europe.

Of course you have the larger situation of cultural or political differences from country to country that influence the church in any given country, but I also found a much smaller problem that ate away at the church in America. It was like termites eating away deep within the structure totally unnoticed. Returning to the States from the front lines of ministry in Europe, I was wounded and needed emergency care. But more importantly, I returned with the images of a lost and hurting world burned into my mind and found an American church that was consumed with itself more than with the world it had been directed to reach.

The Gunnison church that had sent us out had changed pastors while we were in Europe, and it seemed as though we had been forgotten. I used to be the pastor's brother; now the church as a body seemed not to care who I was. Of course, individuals and families within the church knew and prayed for us, and some people supported us financially. But the church as a whole had moved on. The pastor had no idea who we were, and it seemed to me that no one, including the church board, thought it important to tell him about us and our just-completed ministry.

No one asked or perhaps even cared about what we had gone through: out of sight, out of mind. I don't think anyone intended to slight or ignore us as returning missionaries, but we felt as if our work, our time away, our draining experiences meant nothing. It was as if we had never been gone, although to us, much in the church had changed. I think that this is the way it is so many times. Missionaries come home, and no one notices their life-threatening condition. I desperately needed emergency care; instead, it seemed that I received the left foot of fellowship. This church and our friends in it were not equipped to handle my condition. I think that sizes it up fairly: They weren't equipped; they didn't know any better. They had seen the mountain only from one side.

The new pastor was very Pentecostal and seemed to think that the only way to *really* worship God was to shout and dance. I certainly have no problems with people expressing themselves before God any way they want. Even King David danced before the Lord. But when the pastor wanted to force people to worship only in his preferred way, I became uneasy. The new pastor said to do it his way or leave. I knew better. My European experience showed that there are many ways to worship the Lord and that any of them could be beneficial. The ministry of Christ was much too important to squabble over minor issues like this, so in order not to create a disruption in the church, Cindie and I left and sought out a different church to attend.

Ironically, the new church we found ourselves in had a pastor who was very conservative and Baptist in theology. After learning who we were, he wanted me to lead worship for his church. I tried to avoid the inevitable but finally gave in, only then to be accused of trying to force the congregation to become Pentecostal! At the time I thought, *I must be in a good place: They are mad at me from both sides. One side thinks that I am Baptist and the other, that I am Pentecostal.*

Cindie and I returning to the U.S. with a new European look

At the same time, I began to find myself saddened as I learned that our new church was refusing to support one of its own members on the mission field, someone who helped found the church. The reason: difference over a non-essential doctrinal issue.

I was unable to function. It was as if everyone had his or her own view of the mountain and wanted to make sure that everyone else viewed it from only that vantage point. Admittedly, I was not very healthy spiritually and was struggling to survive, but it seemed to me that the church in America was utterly sectarian, devoted to making, not disciples of Christ, but parishioners who agreed with only one view of the mountain: their own!

But what broke my heart the most was seeing how this attitude shaped even American international missions.

One day I was driving up the Interstate and came across a missions organization reaching out to Northern Europe. I was elated to find what I thought would finally be a place of common ground, a place similar to what I had become accustomed to in Europe, where the only important issue was reaching the lost and where other issues would not even be on the radar, so to speak.

I enjoyed meeting the staff. They were all great folks and seemed very sincere in their desire to help a lost continent reach Christ. I gave them my address, and they sent me an application to join their organization. But as I excitedly filled out the application, I came to the last statement at the bottom. It began, "Furthermore...." I kid you not: "Furthermore..." was the exact word that started the statement. It wasn't a question. It was a statement! "Furthermore, we do not accept any applicants who believe in, or practice speaking in tongues." I was dumbfounded.

It could have read just the opposite. It could have read, "Furthermore, we do not accept applicants who do *not* practice or believe in speaking in tongues," and I would have had the same reaction.

What in the world was going on? I thought to myself. *Are we really that simple minded in America? Have we so badly lost sight of the mission field that we can't even see the lost? Do we really care for the lost so little that we would focus on this, instead of them?* Tongues were not the important issue. The fact that it took precedence over lost souls was important!

According to the US Census, over 152,000 people in the world will die and go into eternity as you read this book today! That equals 106 every minute. Only 33% of the world's population is made up of Christians. That would mean that 71 of those who die every minute are not Christians. If you stop and think about it, if you really buy into orthodox Christianity, every time your heart beats, someone goes to hell!

I wonder how many of those people care about a Christian's theological preferences! If a person is standing at the end of the proverbial tunnel, as he faces the gulf between heaven and hell, I am sure he is only saying, "If I had only heard and believed the salvation message!"

Standing on the edge of eternity, they do not care what our theological views are, I am sure. They do not care from which vantage point we view the mountain! If they are lost, I am sure that they wish only that someone would have pointed them in the right direction. But it seems to me that we are often more concerned with our point of view then we are with saving lives first.

I began to believe that the church in America was suffering from a "tunnel vision" Christianity. We are concerned with attracting people to our point of view more than we are with simply pointing them to the mountain, or even taking them by the hand and exploring it together!

I had been in Europe on the mission field, and it seemed to me that all of our denominational and theological differences were not relevant there. People were dying and going to hell. That was the only thing that mattered! On my return to America, it seemed that the American church had simply become a retreat for Christians. We American believers weren't interested in helping others discover the mountain, regardless of the side they approached. We simply wanted to sit and enjoy our view, which we considered to be *the* view.

Needless to say, all of this was more than I could handle spiritually and emotionally. I was experiencing reverse culture shock, and it was too much to bear. I had already lost faith in my dream. And now I became disillusioned with the church in America.

To make matters even worse, it was while we were in Europe that both Jimmy Swaggart and Jim Bakker fell. It was also during this same time that Oral Roberts locked himself in his prayer tower until he died or until someone gave him $8,000,000, whichever came first! On top of that, many other faith healers made national news, not for miracles God had performed, but for questionable or unethical dealings on their part. It really was a poor testimony for Christianity as televangelists faked healings and swindled people. To many observers, the church in America was not looking very Christ-like.

The Christians whom I ran with in Europe scoffed at the American televangelists and their brand of American Christianity so obviously full of self-consuming bells, whistles, lights, and make-up. To the European mind, this type of glitter and guff was not real, and it certainly did not represent the Christianity of the Bible.

Now that I was back in the United States, I began to see the American church in the same light. I didn't see it reaching people for God, but rather providing a comfortable place to distract them from reaching the lost. On top of everything else, reverse culture shock kept me from functioning in this strange new environment that we call American Christianity.

I entered college in Gunnison, Colorado, to earn a Bachelor's degree so that I could teach high school history. Even though, in the beginning, I was motivated by God's love to reach out to young people where they live, I had lost sight of my dream and what I thought was God's plan for my life. Now the father of a newborn, I somewhat suddenly felt the weight of responsibility for food, housing, and clothing land on my shoulders. No more time to chase dreams that ended in heartbreak. Reality stared me in the face, and I found myself angry with God for not fulfilling His end of the bargain. I felt that I had given my all to follow Him and He had let me down. As a result, I entered spiritual and emotional depression. I saw what I had been through as nothing more than a cruel joke. God rescued me for what?—to be *a nobody* who tried and had failed to fulfill his dreams? Some testimony that would be! *If God were not any more faithful than that,* I thought, *He and His calling can just go to hell!* I gave up.

CHAPTER FIVE

Dream

While traveling in Europe with Youth for Christ, I spent many nights in homes of local people who entertained me as their house guest. It was a great experience, and I became acquainted with many "normal" European families. Conversations were plentiful, because they were eager to visit with an American. At the same time, I had the opportunity to learn how Europeans, usually Danes, thought and believed about everything from religion to politics. The evenings almost always ended around the dinner table, having a cup of tea and piece of bread. I have many fond memories of those visits.

Many times my host would make out a bed on the couch in the living room for me to sleep on. The conditions were always comfortable, and my hosts were pleasant people. On some occasions, though, the family would have a grandfather clock in the living room next to where I was trying to sleep. Every hour, on the hour, its loud chimes would strike as many times as the hour. Before midnight I remember praying for 1 a.m. to hurry up and arrive so I would not have to listen to the clock clang ten, eleven, or twelve times. For some reason, on those nights I did not get much sleep!

———

One night, though, while soundly sleeping in a living room, without a grandfather clock, I had a dream that woke me up in a cold sweat. I remember vividly sitting straight up at 5 a.m., terrified by what I had just seen. I wrote the dream down immediately, when I was awakened, because I *knew* it was from God, even though I did not have a clue what it meant.

I dreamed that I was on a ferry boat; actually, it was a ship that held hundreds of people, along with scores of cars and trucks, as they transferred from one island to the next. (This is how I traveled quite regularly, so it was nothing out of the ordinary.) I was out on the deck, while all of the other passengers were up on the bridge having a party with the Captain. Music and laughter rolled off the bridge when someone approached me and invited me up.

"Come on! Everyone is having a good time. Come and join us," he said, holding his drink in a red plastic cup.

I was dumbfounded and not interested. The party on the bridge just seemed to be out of place, and I refused his offer.

As I looked out on the sea, I noticed items floating on the water. As I walked to the bow, I saw people among what I recognized to be the remains of a shipwreck. Some of the people were floating without any flotsam to buoy them, while others clung to bits of wreckage from the destroyed vessel.

Had it been hit and run over by another ship? Maybe even ours, I thought as I struggled to make sense of it. I started yelling for help, but none of the partygoers could hear me. I yelled louder, but no one seemed to even care. They were too busy enjoying the comforts of the bridge party.

Meanwhile, the people in the water, some of them still alive, needed desperately to be rescued. I yelled and screamed for help but no one came.

Finally, I noticed that the ship was changing directions. I instinctively knew that the Captain was trying to change course in order to reach the lost. The only problem was that, as the ship changed course, it began running over the people in the water.

In a sweat of fear, I yelled up to the bridge to stop, but the ship continued, not at a high rate of speed, but steadily nevertheless, methodically plowing over the people in the water. I ran to the edge of the ship and threw out a life line, hoping to rescue at least one. I continued to cry out for help, but no one came.

I remember seeing a young girl in the water grab hold of the rope, and I pulled to raise her to safety. As I pulled, the rope seemed to hang up on something. I struggled all the more to pull the girl to safety, only to be hindered by something keeping me from bringing her on board. Suddenly the rope gave way, and it came up rapidly, as I pulled hand over hand, until I reached the end of the rope. Instead of delivering the young girl, the rope ended noosed around a bloody skull with hair hanging off of only one side. The ship had run her over, pulling her into its powerful propeller. The vessel that should have rescued had killed her instead!

Sitting straight up in bed at 5:00 a.m. in that European living room, I scrambled for a pen and notebook to write down what I had witnessed in my dream. It was too real, too earthshaking, and too relevant to be forgotten. God was trying to tell me something, but what I did not know. What was the ship? What had hurt those people? More importantly, how could those people have been saved? I have struggled with these questions up to the day of this writing.

But when I returned from Europe disillusioned by the church I concluded that the ship must represent the church in America. People outside it are drowning, and many on the ship don't even know it, or maybe even care. Worse, many times it is this ship that runs them over, while trying to save them.

I began to believe that God used that dream to prepare me for what I could not yet comprehend.

When I returned to the United States, I began to see that the American church needed help. Don't get me wrong. I do not claim to be an expert, but my experience in Europe may have given me some insights. When I returned, I could plainly see that the church in America was losing its way. Many people have grown to believe that the church is our sanctuary from the world instead of our vessel into the world. We have become introverted in our perspective and, as a result, are ineffective at doing the very thing God has instituted us to do.

While Americans brag about the "separation of church and state," without realizing it, we are allowing the state to influence our Christianity and cause us to get sidetracked from the Great Commission. Politics influences the church in America more than it does in any nation I have ever witnessed. Never have I heard more sermons about politics than in American evangelical churches. Not only do we American Christians make political decisions because of what the church teaches, but we allow politics to dictate choices that our belief in God should dictate.

Granted, most evangelical Christians may be Republicans, but please don't strike me dead if I say that the Republican Party is not *the* Christian political party. All Democrats are not going to hell! Yet many churches make some people feel that way. If we are not careful, we can become so focused on seeking to enforce our moral convictions through political means (without seeking to transform the heart) that we forget we are dealing with people who resent the condemnation they perceive coming from us. In many cases, we seem to have sacrificed our chance to reach people for Jesus by ostracizing them because of how we express our political views, even when those views concern moral issues about which all Christians should agree. Instead of rescuing people who hold onto different views than ours, we repulse them!

If we are not careful, when we use the church platform as a pulpit to advance our political viewpoint, we can easily alienate ourselves from the very people we should be reaching for Christ. (Not to mention violating the IRS laws!)

I do not believe Jesus wanted to be a politician. That was one reason he was crucified. The Jews wanted a politician to rescue them from the Roman Empire. But Jesus was not a politician, He was a savior! The Jews wanted to be saved from the Romans. Jesus wanted to save them from eternal damnation.

I am afraid that my time in Europe helped to shape my political views, and as a result they no longer coincided with many conservative Christian political views. On the other hand I certainly do not buy into many aspects of the liberal agenda either. As a result, all of this religious political business only aided in the reverse culture shock I was experiencing as I returned to the United States. I have said many times that I am cursed with being a diehard moderate.

While it may be true that the United States is becoming polarized on many political issues, Jesus' own words tell us that he came to save those who are on the other end of the polarization from the church. When Jesus was hanging out with the "wrong" people, Mark tells us in chapter 2:16-17 that,

> *The religion scholars and Pharisees saw him keeping this kind of company and lit into his disciples: "What kind of example is this, acting cozy with the riffraff?" Jesus, overhearing, shot back, "Who needs a doctor: the healthy or the sick? I'm here inviting the sin-sick, not the spiritually-fit.*
> —The Message

We in the church need to have the same attitude as Jesus. But American Christians seem to be retreating. Many of us tend to criticize the other side politically and religiously, never even considering what might have happened to them in the past to cause them to think and behave the way they do. Maybe they have been damaged. Then again, maybe we have been.

The Church culture has become our threat-free space in which we can rail against evil in the world in a performance intended only for other believers. We actually avoid engaging the world that so desperately needs us, so desperately needs God!

Who will represent Christ in the world if all the Christians retreat out of it? Who will ever hear the message if we alienate them by our political statements before we tell them the good news? God's message has to take precedence over our political agenda. We can not get so focused on what we believe that we lose sight of those we are trying to reach. People need to feel rescued, not forgotten, or worse yet, ridiculed!

The lost are drowning, while those who could help to save them are partying on the bridge in the safety of our insulated Christian subculture! It is as if we are not strong enough to engage the dangers of the world. As a result, instead of going into the world as God has commanded us, we retreat to the center of the ship, as far away from the dangerous waters as possible for our own safety.

The point the church needs to teach is, "Of course it is dangerous out there! It will cost you your life!" That is what Christianity is all about. Giving your life away! Dietrich Bonhoeffer said that when Jesus called someone to discipleship, he called them to die. We need not retreat for safety but rather to put on the full armor of God and stand up. Get on our life vest and jump into the water for God's sake. People are dying to know Jesus!

The ship is not for our pleasure cruise; it is God's ferry boat, a working vessel to get us from one place to another. It is truly a safe vessel, but it was never meant to be a luxury liner!

Don't get me wrong. I am not advocating leaving the ship behind. There is safety in the ship. As one person said, "It may have stunk on Noah's Ark, but it was sure better than trying to tread water!" We have to have the ship or we would all be floating aimlessly on the open seas. Even in my state of brokenness and disillusionment when I returned from Europe, as was the case when I was saved as a small child, it was in the church where I ultimately found salvation. Christ instituted the church for the very reason of providing salvation for the lost! Since that is the case, we need to learn how to better use it for that salvation.

God did not ask us to be pew warmers on Sunday mornings, but rather participants in the great event that is taking place out on the seas of life. He called us to go into the world, not to go into a church. If a local church functions properly, "into the world" is where it's going to take its members. So to use a sports analogy from the apostle Paul, we are all great *christ-thletes*! Now, let's get out there and get in the game…for God's sake! At least come off the ship's bridge long enough to look into the water. Once you see, I promise you will never be the same!

CHAPTER SIX

Neighbor

I know of a man who saved all of his money to purchase a home in a very nice neighborhood in the suburbs. The man was raised in a poor family and never had too much in the way of earthly possessions, although he had a strong sense of family. So after moving to the city, he bought a lovely house for his family to enjoy.

The house he purchased, though, had been vacant and neglected for some time and desperately needed some tender loving care. The paint had faded, and the lawn had died. The man immediately set out to repaint the exterior of the house and get the lawn back into shape, to the delight of the neighbors.

But after living in the home for a couple of years, the man received an anonymous letter in his mailbox from someone who said they were neighbors from down the street. Instead of welcoming the man to the neighborhood, the letter complained about how the man mowed his lawn. The envelope had no return address and the typed letter was not signed.

I smiled as I thought of this story because it perfectly illustrates the problem of the church's not being able to interact with the culture it should be reaching for Christ.

I felt sorrier for the writer of the letter than I did the reader. I am not sure if the person who wrote the letter was a Christian or not. There is no way of knowing. If he or she was, their Christianity has not served them very well. On the other hand, if the writer was not a Christian, maybe a good dose of pure Christianity would change the person's attitude about what a neighbor is.

We seem to have lost sight of who our neighbors are. In Jesus' day someone asked Him, "Who is my neighbor?" Today in this highly Christianized American society we seem to no longer even care who our neighbors are.

We climb into metal machines that isolate us from everyone else and leave our homes traveling at a high rate of speed. We fight over who can get to the next intersection first. We return home wrapped in our metal machines and push a button to open our metal doors on the front of our house so we can drive into the garage without ever getting out. The door closes behind us, and we never have to say a word to anyone who might be *our neighbor*. We have successfully isolated ourselves from those around us who might be in need of a friend.

If we have a conflict with one of those *neighbors,* we send them an anonymous letter so we don't have to come into contact with them.

Meanwhile in rural America, seldom a harvest goes by where at least one farmer does not help another get the wheat in before the rains comes or helps him work on his combine so that the harvest can be a success. These farmers may live miles apart, but they are still neighbors. At the same time those of us who have moved into the city hardly know our neighbors who live just a few feet away. To interact with them on a personal level seems totally foreign to us. It is as if by getting closer together, we have drifted farther apart.

Now you tell me: Who is affecting whom more—the church affecting society? Or society affecting the church?

Have the times changed so drastically in America? I can remember my parents helping neighbors on many occasions as I was growing up. I do not remember a Sunday that we did not pick up and take one or more widows to church with us. Mom and Dad always befriended those who lived around us. Our home was always open for company, and we had plenty!

While I was a child in the 1960's, my father was the sheriff in a county that Interstate 40 traveled through. There were many occasions when Dad would come home with a runaway child who should have been spending the night in jail. It seems as though he found these kids in cars speeding down the Interstate heading toward California. Dad always called the child's folks back east somewhere to discover that the child came from a family much like ours and was simply confused and angry. Instead of adding to the child's anger, he brought him or her home to eat dinner and visit with a Christian family, hoping that the child could get a glimpse of how life could be. Then the next day, he would take them to Albuquerque and put them on a plane to go back home. Several of those kids visited my folks years later and thanked them.

In fact at 80 years of age, my parents are still the neighbors everyone longs for. Their Christianity is exemplified in their everyday life. Many people in town still come over to ask Dad's advice on anything from how to fix a car to how to fix a marriage. My mother, even though her health is not what it used to be, is always willing to help at any request.

As I became an adult, I tried to exemplify this same behavior. When Cindie and I were married and bought our first home, I immediately became friends with my neighbors. I helped them with their yard or simply sat on the porch and enjoyed the view of the river with them. Life was simple, and Christianity was lived out in everyday actions.

One elderly neighbor had fallen into the mud in his garden one time, and I went over to help him get up and cleaned off. There were no strings attached. It was just what you were supposed to do. When the same neighbor passed away, the family asked me to sing his favorite song at his funeral in the Catholic Church. After some discussion, the priest finally agreed it would be okay for me, a Protestant, to sing a secular song in his parish.

Several years after I had moved away, this same gentlemen's granddaughter found me on the Internet and asked if I would sing in her wedding in Missouri. I gladly agreed. It was an honor!

But now it is sad to say that many of us in cities know very few of our neighbors personally. We have been trapped in the "metal machine wrapped around the garage door opener" syndrome. Isn't it ironic how, in the city, we are very close in proximity, but miles apart relationally?

It is as if cities represent the problem in many large churches these days. There are so many people so close together that it becomes very difficult to become friends with anyone.

I know of one couple who joined a mega-church, only to stand in the lobby after church on Sunday morning inviting people to go out to lunch, only to be rejected time after time. "In all fairness," you might ask, "why would anyone go out to dinner with a complete stranger? You never know what kind of person you might come across these days." That might be a fair question, but remember we are talking about *church*.

Granted high-quality services at mega-churches have attracted people who would normally never attend church, and lives have been changed. At the same time, how many of us grow into more than just *good-church* attendees? (Emphasis is on "good-church" not good "church attendees.")

Maybe some churches, like some cities, have grown too large for their own good. Like the ship in my dream that ran over its *victims*, we are more concerned with ourselves than the people who need help. Maybe the method in which we are using these ships (churches) is improper. We are using them as gatherers instead of transporters.

There are too many bells; too many whistles; too many *see-it-from-my-point-of-view* thoughts and not enough *"for God so loved the <u>world</u>"* thoughts! We as Christians board the ship for our own pleasures, instead of boarding the ship to reach a destination. Instead of allowing the ship to take us to where God has called us to be, we allow the ship to swallow us alive, and we think that the ship is where we are supposed to be.

How many times have you heard someone say in reference to a church that, "This is just where we feel we're supposed to be right now"? The words, "right now" are the kicker. You would think that those words would indicate the church is taking them into service to a world of hurting people. In reality all they are saying is, "We are going to stay in this church until we go to another one." It is like sailing around in circles going from one ship to another and never arriving at shore, never going to the lost, never even looking out over the water to see if someone is out there crying for help.

How many times do you hear someone say that they changed churches because their needs were not being met at the old church? What is that about? Where do you find that in Scripture? Maybe it would be better stated, "I left that church because I was unwilling to allow it to take me to a destination to work for Jesus." That would be a more correct statement. That is of course assuming the church is actually taking people to a destination to work for Jesus, whether it be inside or outside of the church building.

Remember, the Bible says that it is better to give than to receive. For some reason, many of us go to church just to receive. We have a consumer mentality. Worse yet, many times it is the church in America that has taught us this consumer type of mentality. In many mega-churches today, working in the church has become "for professionals only." Everyone else is supposed to just enjoy the ride. If your quality is not good enough, your job is to watch those perform who project that quality.

Think about it when it comes to church *shopping*. We think, and in many cases are told, that the church is there to give us something. In reality the church should be a tool to help us achieve God's plan! How can people learn God's plan if they are never given the chance and the responsibility to practice it?

Here's an idea! Instead of a church going door-to-door witnessing to get people to come to church, why not go door-to-door witnessing *not* to ask the person living there for anything? Maybe we should just say, "Hi. My name is Gene McMath, and I don't want anything!" No strings! No invitations to come to our church. Nothing! Go door-to-door witnessing just to give. Now there's a concept! I can say that because it is not my idea. Remember, "For God so loved the world that he *gave*...." It might be like taking a life boat to drowning victims! Let's try it. Walk over to your neighbors' house, and knock on the door just to say, "Hi." Make a friend for God's sake. Not to get anything from them, but just to offer them friendship.

We need to live a better life instead of trying to force others to. We need to live a life that is more giving and less demanding. We must learn to live our life so others see Jesus in us. That is what the Great Commission is all about.

In order for that to happen, we cannot isolate ourselves from our neighbors. Or, to borrow from an earlier chapter, we cannot be more concerned with our view of the mountain than we are with simply showing other people the way to reach it. The next time you come home from church and pull up to your drive, reaching for your garage-door opener in order to go into your house without ever seeing another person, stop and ask yourself: "How may I show Christ to my neighbors in a practical way?" That is where true Christianity is lived out.

Like the people in my dream drowning in the water or the person who sent the anonymous letter from just down the street, everyone needs to be reached out to. Everyone needs a neighbor. Whose neighbor are you?

CHAPTER SEVEN

Dying

Think of yourselves the way Christ Jesus thought of himself. He had equal status with God but didn't think so much of himself that he had to cling to the advantages of that status no matter what. Not at all. When the time came, he set aside the privileges of deity and took on the status of a slave, became human! Having become human, he stayed human. It was an incredibly humbling process. He didn't claim special privileges. Instead, he lived a selfless, obedient life and then died a selfless, obedient death....

—Philippians 2:5–8 The Message

As I returned home from Europe, I could see clearly that the church in America was hurting. It was very easy for me to see that the ship was floundering and that if someone didn't do something we were going to capsize. Once again I began to yell and scream for help (not literally, of course), but no one would listen. It was as if, I thought, no one wanted to hear. I was angry at God for letting me down, and then I became critical of the church.

I remember standing on the front steps of a Baptist church with a good friend of mine who was the pastor. He spoke gently to me and said, "Gene, I am concerned for you. You seem to be very angry at the church. The church is the body of Christ, and you are not in a good position when you are angry at His body."

I tried desperately to convey to him that I was not angry at Christ's body. The body of Christ is precious and made up of people who are called out by Him and Him alone. The body of Christ is made up of those who truly see and understand the things of God. The members of the body of Christ use their personal devotional time to draw themselves into a relationship with God, not just their church services and Christian events. The body of Christ is made up of all those individuals who have a living faith in Christ, who should be in fellowship with a local group of members, and who yet still live as though they are missionaries right where they live.

"What I was angry with, what I was disillusioned with," I continued to explain "was this institution that man has created in America. This farce we call Christianity! This institutionalized church business that has become a party ship that gathers people for its own consumption rather than a working vessel that transports people to their calling!"

I was obviously a hurting individual. I felt as though God had let me down. I felt as though the church had let me (and God) down. When people hurt, they tend to draw a line and say that God is on their side, while they lash out at others. Well, I couldn't quite put my finger on the source, but I knew that I had been hurt, and now I was lashing out!

I once had a dog named Princess. She was a beautiful full-bred Collie. She had a pedigree a mile long. She was very gentle and precious, calm as could be. And, I think, she loved me more than anybody in the world. I would play with her, throw sticks for her to retrieve, roll around on the grass with her, as well as bathe and brush her. She was incredible! We were the best of buds! But one day Princess was run over by a pickup.

She wasn't killed but hurt badly enough that she sat there on the road with her hind end stuck to the pavement as though she had sat down on super glue. Meanwhile her front end tried to go around in circles on her front feet! First looking one direction and then another as though she was trying to go somewhere. I knew instinctively that she was looking for me to come and help. At least I thought she was! I ran over to try to help her, and before I knew it she snapped at me. At me! I was her best friend, her protector; the one who fed her, played with her, took care of her. I did nothing to hurt her. I was only there to help, and yet she acted as though I was the source of the problem! Who knows why dogs act that way? You would think that they would cherish help from the one they love the most and the one who loves them the most. But for some reason, when hurt, they snap at their master.

I understood the situation. I knew that she was confused and in severe pain. So I worked with her until she knew I was not the source of her pain. I could not leave her there in the middle of the road. That would have been deadly. Another automobile would have come and run her over. I had to move her. If she would only allow me to help, even though it might hurt even more for a short time, I could save her life. She was too precious not to save!

I wonder if God feels the same way about us. Maybe God even hurts for us. I know I was hurting for Princess in the middle of that road. I couldn't feel her pain or anything, but it hurt when she snapped at me. God must look down and hurt for us every day. We fall so short and make so little use of our God-given potential. We sit on our hind ends going nowhere, looking for someone else to save us, and all the while not allowing them to.

The pain that I felt at the bottom of the cliff when I had my accident in 1983 in no way compared to the emotional hurt I was going through at this time in my life. I had returned home from Europe broken. I needed emergency care, and everywhere I turned for any semblance of healing and protection seemed to let me down. I found myself alone and hurting almost more than I could bear. I became angry at any- and everything around me. People tried to help, and I ended up hurting them. I did not mean or want to hurt people, but like a dog injured after being hit by a car, when someone came close to help, I snapped!

When I was much younger, before the accident, I use to preach that if our eyes were not on Jesus then we were in sin. I believed that Jesus had all the answers and we needed to just focus on Him. He would provide our every need and salvation in the present time of trouble. Some would even add that it is wise to deny you have any trouble. "Don't admit it. Don't recognize it. Satan is a liar and a thief who will destroy you, if you let him."

The only problem is, in reality we as humans do not have what it takes to overcome troubles on our own. Faking it ultimately does not solve the problem. When we pretend we don't have any problems, everyone around us sees us better then we see ourselves. Jesus sees us, and he is not fooled. He knows. We need help!

Ultimately I learned through this hurting time that God does want to supply all our needs, but it does not always come in the clean, neatly wrapped package we think it should come in. Sometimes there are natural consequences. God uses these natural consequences to help us grow. I thought that when I was at the bottom of that cliff I had hit bottom. Now I was learning that *bottom* is down much farther than just at the end of a fall.

Emotional, psychological, and spiritual injuries that go unnoticed deep below the surface can be much more devastating than any outward injury. I had been wounded more deeply by the mission field than I could have ever imagined. The injuries left from the truck wreck paled in comparison!

I was now truly at bottom!

When you are at bottom, you have no choice but to look up. And when you do look up, you will find that God sees you and knows where you are. He saw me and knew where I was. He saw a lost, hurting little child who needed some attention. God is like that. He sees what we need, not what we want. I wanted to become famous, and it almost killed me. God saw what I needed. He saw that I needed to become a nobody.

God can use a nobody. He cannot use people who long to be somebody. If we are willing to lose our lives and give up and let Him rescue us from certain destruction, then we will each find a life that is so fulfilling that we cannot contain the excitement. God was teaching me how to lose my life so I could find the one He had for me.

As I write this sentence, we are taking our oldest daughter, Stina, away to live at college. She was born in Europe and was 22 days old when we returned to the United States.

I remember that our flight was delayed in Copenhagen, Denmark, for several hours. As a result, we missed our connection in New York City. So when we arrived in New York, we were forced to spend the night there and catch a different flight the next day that took us through St. Louis.

On that flight every seat was taken. When we flew over the Atlantic from Denmark, we had an empty seat in which we were able to lay Stina. Now there were no empty seats, and Stina did not like sitting on my lap as I sat still in my seat.

I am not sure if you have ever been on a plane with a screaming baby, but it is not enjoyable, especially if the baby is not yours! So out of courtesy to the other passengers, I got up and walked up and down the aisles carrying Stina the whole flight in order to keep her from crying.

To this day, I still remind her that I walked all the way from New York City to St. Louis in order to get her back home. She was worth the walk!

I will allow you to personalize that story. For me, I can hear God saying, "Remember when I walked up that hill just outside the gates of Jerusalem. *You were worth the walk!*"

God is willing to do whatever it takes to get us to where He has called us to be. It may hurt. It may cause discomfort. It may even call for sending us away from home for a time. But in the end, His goal is to save us. His goal is to make us like Him, one concerned with others more than we are with ourselves. He wants to bring us home. In order to go home, it takes a journey. Now I realize God was taking me on a journey!

I spent the next three-and-a-half years after returning from Europe going to college so I could teach high school in the United States. This was nothing more than completing my undergraduate degree. But when you add in the "life factor," it was momentous.

As I mentioned, Stina was just a newborn, so Cindie and I took turns taking care of her. I would get up at 4:00 a.m. to throw newspapers and then at 8:00 a.m. go to class until noon. After that I would come home to do homework and take care of Stina while Cindie went to work.

As is the case with most college students, we made very little money during this time. In fact if you were to check our tax records, I am sure that we made around $4000.00 during *one* of those four years. That was the *most* money we made in any given year while I was in school. We survived on very little.

We were so short on money that I was not even able to afford a costume for Stina during Halloween. As you can imagine, I was not feeling very good about my "dad capabilities." A dad is supposed to be the provider for his family. Because of the situation during this time, I felt like I was not doing a very good job.

Thank God for Cindie! She was the essence of stability. Not only did she stand firm, as she had through the entire ordeal of the accident, but once again she was keeping me alive with prayer and support. When I couldn't afford to buy a Halloween costume, she made one out of items around the house. To this day, over fifteen years later, that costume is the one that Stina remembers—and maybe even liked—the most! When I was unable to hold things together, Cindie was glue. When I was crumbling, she was a rock.

Selah as a baby, with her older sister Stina

Before we left for Denmark, I did everything I could to sell our little house on the river, but for some reason it just wouldn't sell. Some friends said that God wouldn't let us sell it. If that was true, now I knew why: That home was all we had when we returned. We lived in that little house and became a family, even though times were rough, almost more than I could bear. At least we had a place to live.

As I was about to graduate, Selah, our second child, was born. It was a very difficult time. By this time I was suffering from depression, and, to be quite honest, I wanted to die.

A few years later, when Selah was about six years old, I was backing out of the garage. I was busy pushing the button to close the garage door and putting the car in reverse to back out and then into first gear to leave as I got to the street. While all this was going on, Selah sat in the back seat with her seat belt on saying, "Daddy, put on your seat belt."

I had been so busy doing everything that I had not yet gotten around to it. I have always worn my seat belt since that night when I drove off the cliff. On that night I was not wearing a seat belt and it saved my life because I was thrown out of the truck. Statistics say that you have about a one in a million chance of surviving an accident like that if you are not wearing your seat belt. I figure that I used up my one chance, so now I always wear my seat belt.

At any rate I had not yet put on my seat belt, and Selah kept saying, "Daddy, put on your seat belt."

Finally I reached over and snapped my seat belt into place. Selah let out a sigh of relief and said, "Daddy, I just may have saved your life!"

I looked into the mirror at that beautiful little blond-headed girl with bright blue eyes and thought to myself that she must have come into the world to bring me something from God. I thought back to her birth while I was in that state of depression. I thought of how I was angry and wanting to die, and then she was born so fragile and yet so full of life. I remembered how I was a mess but she was precious. I paused for a moment as these thoughts raced through my mind, and then I simply smiled and said, "Yes, Selah, you just may have saved my life."

For my last semester in college, I had to student teach. For some reason, I was unable to student teach in Gunnison and had to go to another town about eighty miles away! Now I was forced to live in a garage apartment, for which I was very thankful, but without Cindie, who stayed in Gunnison to work and give birth to Selah. Life was not easy!

On top of all of that, I had stopped leading worship at church, not on the best of terms. My dreams of playing music and being a recording artist were totally dead. Life sucked, and I no longer cared. I entered situations that were destructive and only made matters worse. I was fighting for my life and destroying it at the same time.

As I look back on it, I realize how obvious it was that I would be in such emotional pain! I had gone from the bottom of a cliff to the heights of a dream in four short years. Then I followed that up by completing a four-year degree, with student teaching, in only three and one-half years. I graduated near the top of my class with a GPA of 3.85. I had poured my life out! Now, it was all over. My dream, my schooling, and, as I saw it, my life, were coming to an end, all pretty much at the same time! I lost hope. When a person loses hope, life itself is threatened. I saw no hope, no future. All I had worked for was gone. It was hopeless. I was hopeless. I died!

We relocated to Hugo, an extremely small town on the Eastern Plains of Colorado, which was an aspect of dying for me. Not only was I forced to leave all my dreams and goals behind, but we were also leaving our home in the mountains, the only semblance of a home we ever had in our married years. Our life, my life, as I knew it, had come to an end.

The only problem was that dying was exactly what I needed to do! The old Gene needed to die so God could resurrect a new one. One that would become less selfish, less self-centered. I guess God always knows what we need. God knew what I needed, and He basically forced it upon me. Leaving the mountains of Colorado meant that I was also making a final decision of placing Cindie and my family above my own selfish desires. Sometimes when dreams die, life arises.

Living in the Eastern Plains of Colorado proved to be the best six years of my adult life. It was there that I began to be content in whatever state I found myself. God had seemed to place me on the shelf, and that was just fine with me. I bought a little house and began to make a home for my family. I became the head high school football coach, taught history, and was simply a husband and a father. I no longer needed to do great things. I was content to stay there for the rest of my life.

I went into the back yard and placed stakes in the ground to mark where the sun was shining at any given time of the day. I had determined to build onto the back of the house so that it would become a home for us to raise our children. I wanted the sun to shine in the house

Gene on top of the rafters while building the house in Hugo, Colorado

at all hours of the day to help stave off the depression. That house turned out to be our dream home.

It had a sunken living room and three bedrooms. I loved being able to sit in any window and enjoy the sun coming in. It was a home fit to stay in for the next twenty years. I had managed to build a home to raise our family.

When we first moved to that small town on the Eastern Plains, I noticed the grave yard next to the highway just outside of town. I remember thinking to myself that I did not want to be buried there. It was just a pasture full of wild native grass with headstones sticking up. It was then that it dawned on me that "home is where you want to be buried." I realized that I was a man without a home.

I now say from time to time that building that house was the most spiritual thing I ever did. I was willing to spend the rest of my life there in that little town on the Eastern Plains of Colorado. I became totally willing to go nowhere and be a nobody for Christ. I never even thought about the dreams of the past or the music career. I was no longer chasing after something. I was just being a husband and a dad. I was just *being*. Not that I had it all together, but I was content. I was even willing to be buried in that graveyard should I die there.

That is when I heard a whisper in my ear. Once I was content; once I wanted nothing; once it was no longer about Gene McMath; once the dream only consisted of what God wanted and not what I wanted; once I let it all go, not just making a conscious choice, but when I didn't even think of it any more because it really no longer mattered to me— that is when I heard God say, "Now I can use you."

CHAPTER EIGHT

Storm

In the fall of 1997, God began to tug on my heart once again to leave my teaching career in Colorado and follow Him in a new and unknown direction. Later that school year, in March of 1998, I wrote,

> *There is a great storm looming directly in front of me. I perceive hardship, distress, troubles, and problems on every hand, yet still I must go forward. For somewhere in the midst of that storm is my salvation.*

It all began with a 61-14 loss in the state playoffs. I was fortunate enough to turn the high school football team into a state contender after four years. By the time we were in our sixth year, we had become district champions. We went into the state playoffs as the number one seed from our district, playing number three from another district.

The biggest blizzard of the year came the night before we were supposed to play. If you have ever been on the Eastern Plains of Colorado in a blizzard, you know that conditions can be terrible. As a result, the game was postponed for three days until the storm had passed and the field could be cleaned off. It all went downhill from there. By the time the game was over, *we* were the ones being cleaned off of the field.

The football season had ended abruptly and unexpectedly. I left the locker room heartbroken, got into my old pickup, and drove home. When I walked into the front door, Cindie stood holding a brochure. It was for a college weekend at Oral Roberts University in Tulsa, Oklahoma.

Now I was standing in my living room with no excuse. It did not look like I would be coaching any more football games that year, as the numbers 61-14 flashed before my eyes!

In the summer prior to that football season, I ran into Dr. Jerry Horner in the parking lot of New Life Church in Colorado Springs. Dr. Horner was the Dean of The School of Theology and Missions at Oral Roberts University. I spoke with him briefly about myself and the future. He gave me some advice and without incident we parted.

I had come across Ted Haggard, pastor of New Life Church, several years earlier, when my father-in-law, Walt, purchased a business in Colorado Springs. The town was full of, for lack of better words, "evil spirits." I hated Colorado Springs in those days. It just seemed dark and gross. I never wanted to live there, and it was tough even spending time there helping to get the business going.

I remember standing on the third floor of his business one night watching teenagers taunt a car they had trapped. As I watched, I saw the kids begin to pelt the car with rocks. One of the rocks crashed through the side window as the confused driver tried to escape. The only way the car could get away was to break the law and continue the wrong way down a one way street.

It was at this same time that Ted moved to Colorado Springs and witnessed the same type of spiritual warfare. The only difference was that instead of hating the town and not wanting to live there, he moved there to start New Life Church. In fact, not long after that night's event, Ted taught a Bible study in that same building in which I was standing.

I was not involved with Ted or his ministry at all during that time. But a few years later, after I had spent time in Europe, returned home, suffered from depression, and given up on church, my father-in-law introduced me to Ted personally. By this time, New Life Church was a couple of thousand people large.

Although I am sure that there were many, many others who were fulfilling God's commission, God used Ted to show me that the institutionalized American church could actually do what God had called it to do. Probably more than anything else, this new conviction turned my life around for God. New Life was the first mega-church I had ever attended. And for the first time ever I had come across a church and a pastor who were actually doing what I felt God had called the church to do.

Unfortunately, the events that you will read about at the end of this book are also affected by Ted. I am writing this just days after watching his life and ministry crumble before a national audience in 2007. I stood there staring at the television, watching a news crew from Denver interview him in his driveway. Listening to the inflection of his voice, it was too obvious. I looked at him on TV and said with a broken heart, "Ted, you are lying." I thought of how many times he had said to me, as well as to audiences around the world, "There is no such thing as a secret. Either everyone already knows or will know." As I was making difficult decisions later, this sad event, although in no way causing my decisions, helped to motivate and shape the events that will bring this book to a close.

By the time New Life Church was a few years old, I had many friends who had been members from its beginning. On Sunday evenings from time to time, we would go into Colorado Springs from our eastern Colorado town and visit. I had the chance to visit with Ted several times during conferences and during church services, so by now he was at least familiar with my face. It was during one of these conferences that I ran into Dr. Horner in the parking lot.

A few months later, on a Sunday night after service, I was visiting with the worship leader, Ross Parsley. As I told him that I felt like I needed to go to Oral Roberts University to earn a Master's in Theology but was scared and not quite sure if I should do it, Ted came up and sat down next to me. After hearing my thoughts, Ted looked right at me and said,

"You have no choice. You need to go to Tulsa. There is nothing to lose. If it doesn't work out, you can just come back here. If you don't go, you will always wonder what would have happened if you did."

I had never been an Oral Roberts fan, but thought, *Well, Ted turned out okay. So, I guess I could give it a try.*

We made reservations, and in two weeks I found myself in Tulsa, taking a graduate entrance exam. Other visitors at the college weekend asked with excitement if I was "going to go for it."

My answer was always the same. "I will just take one step at a time and see what door God provides for me to walk through." There were no emotions and very little excitement. There was only a need to move forward.

While we were in Tulsa for the college weekend, a doctor at the university gave us the name of a realtor that we might like to use if we chose to buy a home there. When we returned to Tulsa for a visit the following spring, we contacted the realtor and started looking at houses.

We looked from one end of town to the other, only to be frustrated by not knowing where we should live. We were not sure where we wanted our two elementary-age girls to go to school or where we would find jobs. The thought of moving to the city from our safe little town in Eastern Colorado was more than we could comprehend.

After returning home from Tulsa, I applied to matriculate in the fall of 1998. If my test scores were high enough and I was accepted, I would take it as a sign that God had opened the door. From there I would "keep walking" and see what God wanted next. This was easy, because all of the pressure was on God. If I was not accepted, then I could go my own way and be at peace. I had followed God's leading and He had closed the door. I had done my part, and God had done His. No problem!

Then I received the letter: I had been accepted. Now what?

Okay, I can handle this, I thought. *I'll just put my house up for sale. We have to sell our house if we expect to move to Tulsa.* So I made a deal with God. If He would sell our house, I would resign my job and go to Tulsa. *Simple enough,* I thought to myself. *If God does His part, I'll do mine.* We proceeded to get the house ready to sell.

My oldest daughter, Stina, who was now in fourth grade, found a for-sale sign and nailed it up to a tree in the front yard. That is when all hell broke loose, literally. Rumors of every kind started. And I heard them all (I think). Some of them were even true! I had to answer questions from my students and fellow teachers everyday. My response was always; "I'm just taking it a step at a time." I never confirmed nor denied that I was quitting my teaching and coaching jobs, or leaving. I didn't know. Besides, I had made a deal with God about selling our home. He had not yet come through with His end of the bargain. We had advertised our house in the papers but as of yet had no response.

The storm loomed.

While in Tulsa, the realtor had asked Cindie what she did for a living. When Cindie said that she was a travel agent, he asked her for a résumé. His wife was a department head for a major air carrier in Tulsa, and he thought that she might help Cindie get a job. She passed Cindie's résumé among the other department heads.

A couple of months after we returned to Colorado, the airline called and asked if Cindie would be interested in interviewing for a position. They flew her to Tulsa, interviewed her, and offered her a job. We were dumb-founded. That is not at all the deal I had made with God.

Now what should we do? Cindie had "a dream job" in Tulsa, but I still had a teaching job, and we still owned a home in Colorado. This all started out so that I could go to school to study for a Master's in Theology. God was not playing within the rules. I had it all figured out and told Him what I needed in order to accomplish this endeavor for Him, but His return was more powerful then my serve. God had put the ball back in my court.

He was showing me that I was the one who was going to have to take a leap of faith and trust in Him, not the other way around. There was no need for Him to take a leap of faith. He already trusted in me. "Would I trust in Him?" was the question. So, I leaped!

Cindie accepted the position, and I resigned my teaching job. We were moving to Tulsa even if the house did not sell. As it turned out the person who took my teaching job also bought our house. Once again God's faithfulness was greater than my faith. If I had not trusted in Him and resigned my job, the people who bought our home would never have moved to town. Our house would not have sold and we would still be living in it today. It took my trusting in God's faithfulness before He could show His unfailing compassion for our well being.

We still had not purchased a home in Tulsa, and, as I mentioned earlier, this was not an easy task. Moving to the city with our two little girls was a scary matter. I placed a map of the city of Tulsa on the floor and told God that I needed His help. Through prayer and some research, a square mile block seemed to lift off of the map. I knew that this was where we were supposed to live. I know that sounds kind of strange. To think, as if God really cared which block we lived in. But then again we were like little children needing the guidance of a father.

I called the realtor and described the house I wanted, where I wanted it, and the price I could pay. The realtor told me that it would not be easy to find what I had described. The best elementary school in that school district was in that block. Therefore, people were willing to pay more for homes there. Two hours later the realtor called back and faxed the description of a house that had just come onto the market. It was exactly the house I had described, for the price that I said I could pay. We moved into that home, and our girls walked the whole way to school on a green belt. It was even better than we could have imagined. Sure enough God the Father demonstrated that he cared for us.

The McMath family in front of their new home in Tulsa, Oklahoma

I began attending the School of Theology and Missions at Oral Roberts University. I still did not know where God was taking me or what I would do once I arrived there. But once again I began to understand that God had a plan for my life.

Early on in my studies, I remember sitting in one of the large amphitheater lecture rooms at the school thinking, "*Wow! I cannot believe I am sitting here, taking classes at Oral Roberts University.*" It was surreal to me. To think that God would still take time out of eternity to care for me. I was overwhelmed with the thought that He must *really* care for me. I learned things about the church, history, and theology that inspired me beyond words. The professors at the school are incredible!

God proved to be more faithful than I could comprehend. In one class called Introduction to Missions, we studied missionary writings of all kinds. Some told of life on the mission field, others of life as missionaries after returning home to their mother country. They spoke of hardships both going and coming that went along with the rewards of serving God as missionaries.

It was in this class that I realized for the first time since returning from Europe that I was a missionary casualty. I learned that I was not alone. There are many missionaries who return from the mission field so beaten and battered that they can not function. God used seminary to simply teach me that He saw me and knew where I was.

One day while walking up the long sidewalk to class, I noticed a fellow graduate student, who was a single mom, trying to get her 5-year-old son out of a bush. Being an energetic, inquisitive boy, he had automatically climbed into it to play. At the same time, the mom was trying to wipe her 6- year-old daughter's nose with her handkerchief, all the while struggling to keep her books and papers from flying away in the wind.

I calmly reached over and held the boy's hand to lead him to her and said, "This is really what it's all about, isn't it?" She smiled as if to agree, and I realized, maybe more than she, that ministry was much more than just *doing church*.

God was teaching me about humanity while I thought I was learning about Theology. He was showing me that He had not forgotten about me. God still loved me. He still loves all of us and has not forgotten. He sees us where we are.

As automatically as my heart would beat or my lungs would inhale, I found myself saying over and over again, "I am so thankful!" God had truly restored hope to a man who had once been broken! He made me into a totally different person than who I used to be when I was living in depression. He saved me.

Because of my teaching experience, I was a Graduate Assistant, teaching for the undergraduate theology department. I began to entertain the idea of being able to teach full time at Oral Roberts University upon graduating. I mentioned it to a few people and waited to see what would happen.

After completing most of my Master's work and petitioning to graduate, Dr. Thomson Mathew, the new Dean of the School, invited me into his office and asked me to consider accepting the position as Representative for the School of Theology and Missions. After praying about it and discussing the matter with Cindie, I took on the position as the school's Representative. Just a few years earlier, I had given up on the American institutional church. Years earlier I had scoffed at American televangelists. Now I found myself right in the middle of it all.

Have you ever noticed that the only ones complaining about the water temperature at the pool are the ones who are not in the water? Well, God was telling me to jump in, the water was fine. I had no idea what God was doing to me, but without even realizing it, I was being restored.

I began to get glimpses of the meaning of the dream I had while traveling in Europe. I had not even spoken of, or thought about, that dream for many years. But now, without even realizing it, God was teaching me a lesson.

While I was studying in seminary and working for the University, I began to realize how people feel a call to serve God "full time" and, as a result, end up in the middle of the church ship I wrote about earlier, never to see another lost person again. I became sad as I realized that the church system we have in America creates ship dwellers, when it should be creating search and rescue teams.

That is what I liked about Ted Haggard, without even realizing it. Ted and New Life Church represented a group of people who were actually involved in their community. I saw them as people who were doing search and rescue in their everyday lives. Not some kind of sub-culture Christians, but ordinary people doing ordinary things and achieving extraordinary results.

I know that when people go to school to gain expertise in a specific field, enrollment in that school will include a much higher percentage of persons seeking that expertise than one will find in the world at large. For instance, in business school nearly all students will be seeking to be senior officers in companies and corporations. In law school, nearly all students aim to be lawyers. But I had a difficult time believing that everyone attending seminary at Oral Roberts University truly needed to be a pastor! In fact I heard one person say, "We could win the world for Christ if we could just keep all of you from going into the ministry!"

It seemed to me that everybody studying at the seminary level wanted to be a ship captain. In reality I believe what God needs is "all hands on deck!" Jesus said to pray for workers to go into the harvest, not to go into the church! I guess every ship needs a captain, but I could not see why so many of us were captains needing a ship.

I don't know. I'm not sure if it is just the way I see things, or if it is the calling God has placed on my life, but for some reason I began to look for the life boats. The party was going strong on the bridge, but I wanted to jump ship and get into the water! I thought to myself, *Maybe I am one of those students who does not need to be a pastor.* As a missionary friend once told me, "Gene, the mission field has ruined you. You can no longer do church as normal." So I began to look for a way to go back "into the world" and represent Christ on what I believed to be His terms.

I used to say that if our eyes were not on God, then we were in sin. Now I say that God wants us to climb up onto His lap and look at the world from His point of view. If we as Christians could only see what He sees, I am sure our viewpoint would be much different! I found that I would rather be discussing life with sinners than God with Christians. So, as I was completing my Master of Arts in Theology and graduating with a 4.00 GPA, I decided to return to the public sector as a high school history teacher, only to discover God was not yet through with me. He was about to solidify my return from brokenness. He had one more lesson that He needed me to experience so that I knew I had been totally rescued from the bottom of a cliff.

CHAPTER NINE

Hiatus

While I was representing the School of Theology and Missions at Oral Roberts University, a man walked into my office to ask some questions about attending there. His name was Blaine Herron. As we visited, I learned that he was a graduate from Life Pacific College in California and was now pastor of a Foursquare church in a town about 90 miles away from Tulsa.

As Blaine and I sat and visited, I knew God had put him in my path. I had never attended a Foursquare Church in my life, but for some reason, all of a sudden I came across someone I clicked with. I asked him as many questions about the Foursquare Church as he asked me about the university. God was conniving.

On the very first weekend I attended Oral Roberts University, I met a man in front of the elevator who was in charge of the Doctor of Ministry program. It turned out that this man worked for the school at the invitation of Dr. Jerry Horner, the same person who had given me advice at New Life Church a year or two before.

As we visited there at the elevator, I discovered that he was from Albuquerque, New Mexico, not far from where I grew up. I learned that he helped to start Hope High School, a school that was one of our high school sports competitors. As was the case with Blaine, this man and I also clicked.

One day after speaking for Blaine at his church, I mentioned to him that I thought a new Foursquare Church had been started in Tulsa. He looked in his denominational directory and said, "Yes, that is true. The pastor's name is Dan Hedges"—the man I had met at the ORU elevator!

After finishing the last class I ever took at Oral Roberts University, my professor, Dr. Roy Hayden, approached me and said, "You know we have started a new Foursquare Church and need a worship leader. Why don't you come by the church and see if you are interested." Guess who the pastor was: Dr. Dan Hedges!

After graduating from ORU and returning to being a history teacher, I ended up leading worship at that church. It seemed as though there was something bigger in the works than I could see. God was on the move again. My only responsibility was to follow.

While leading worship there, I learned that the national Foursquare church was launching a "Multiplication

Process," with the goal of doubling the number of Foursquare churches both inside and outside the United States. Foursquare is a very missions-minded denomination and has many more churches outside of the United States than it does inside. Being such a missions-minded organization, some leaders wanted to start some post-modern churches in America—part of a movement of Emerging Churches that would engage post-modern people, especially the unchurched and post-churched. Churches that actually reach into the world in which it lives instead of asking the world to cross the cultural barrier to reach into the church subculture.

It did not take very long for me to jump on the proverbial bandwagon. Here was the opportunity to minister through the local church the way I believed God had taught me through our experiences as musical missionaries in Europe. I began to recruit a church plant team to start a post-modern church in Tulsa, Oklahoma.

The first members of the team were, of course, my family. Cindie actually volunteered in a coffee shop to learn how to make mochas and lattés so she could serve people when they came to church. Stina agreed to play the keyboard on the worship team. Selah turned out to be an incredible help with insights and positive suggestions even at her very young age of ten. It was truly a family effort. We viewed it as though we were going to go on the mission field without ever leaving home! Soon other families joined in. Before long we had a group made up of several families, as well as a few singles.

The southern part of the United States is referred to as the Bible belt. If you are not familiar with Tulsa, Oklahoma, people refer to it as the buckle of the Bible belt. Or, as I put it, Tulsa is the pit in the arm of Christ. That would make it the arm pit of Christ! If you are a Charismatic, faith-seeking, healing agent of God, Tulsa is your ship, but not a very post-modern place, as far as churches are concerned.

We, as well as other Foursquare leaders, contemplated starting this new church in another town, but I had remembered the day driving down the road, when I heard God say, "Gene, you thought that I brought you to Tulsa for your ministry, but in reality I brought you here for your family." I had uprooted them to leave all that we knew in Colorado to come to Tulsa, and I was not going to uproot them again. Besides, I knew that if I was going to affect the church in a positive way, I had to be right in the middle of it. I could not affect it from the outside.

So after two years of leading worship, we started a post-modern church called The Journey in Tulsa, Oklahoma, right in the middle of the American-tel-evangelist-mega-church scene, or as some people call it "Tulsarusalem." The ship once again was turning, and I was taking notice! To me it was "All hands on deck!"

We moved tables, couches, and chairs into the "sanctuary." In reality it would not be a sanctuary at all, in the traditional sense. What we pictured was more of a night club setting. Not only did we place tables for visitors, family, and friends, but we brewed coffee and served snacks in the meeting area. We hoped to make Journey meetings more relevant to people who never really liked going to church. We thought that the comfortable atmosphere would help change the way people saw church.

I think that perhaps we in Tulsa are so interested in the things of God that many topics we talk about from the pulpit cannot even be understood by everyday people. So, I spoke plainly in an ordinary tone of voice, using stories and words that everybody could understand. I tried to make people feel like they didn't need to be a theologian or Bible scholar to attend church, which was not too hard for me to do! Even with a Master's in Theology, I do not claim to be a theologian. After all, who really understands the mind of God!

We wanted Journey meetings not to be sterile religious gatherings, but rather "happening" events full of excitement, with a lot going on. People would be busy moving around, visiting and enjoying each other. We would no longer use terms such as preachers and sermons; instead, people would speak of narrators and discussions. In fact I did not even want to be known as the pastor. Sure, that may be a gifting God gives people, but to me it carried too many unhelpful cultural connotations.

Many postmodern thinkers are turned off by the image they conjure up when they hear the term "pastor." It is certainly not usually the case, and most pastors are very caring individuals who give their life to help others, but to many postmodern thinkers, the word *pastor* represents, at best, a person that you could not be yourself around because he might tell God on you or something, and, at worst, someone decked out in a three-piece suit, hair slicked back, powerful microphone in hand, scheming to get your money! That certainly is not me, and I did not want to be put into either one of those categories! We wanted desperately to separate ourselves from any mindset that would create a chasm between us and the unchurched. We just wanted to be real. In fact what we were trying to do, for lack of better terminology, was to start an *unchurch*.

We hoped that people who never went to church but who longed somehow to make contact with the Creator would come, bring their families, sit around tables, and enjoy other people. We wanted people to build relationships with one another while they listened and sang contemporary songs that they could hear on the radio during the week. Journey meetings would entertain and yet challenge with relevant talks and discussions along with dramas, skits, and other creative ministry.

Finally, we hoped that people who had given up on going to church could find a place where they could come together and worship God. As a result, I thought more and more people would be drawn to Christ through a culturally relevant approach. People would come to The Journey and fellowship with friends with whom they would also spend time during the week.

The McMath family on a mission trip with The Journey

At least that was our goal! And in many cases it did work that way, but on a much smaller scale than I had hoped.

Our second goal was to help Christians in Tulsa realize the importance of relationships with those who were not followers of Christ: to help them get out of the bridge in the middle of the ship and take a look out over the water. I struggled to find ways to make this happen. We wanted "real life stuff" that encouraged people to build relationships with each other centered upon the common interests that God had placed in their lives.

Those common interests would be the starting point for witnessing to unbelieving friends.

About eighteen months into The Journey I wrote an article that was published on www.CPforum.net: "Getting the Churched out of the Church." It reads as follows:

GETTING THE CHURCHED OUT OF THE CHURCH
by Gene McMath, Pastor

The Journey Foursquare Church—Tulsa, OK

In *SoulTsunami*, Leonard Sweet writes, "Postmodern evangelism doesn't say to the world, 'come to church.' Rather, it says to the church, 'go to the world.'"
We at The Journey in Tulsa, OK are trying to achieve that very same objective.

In our short 18-month existence we are realizing that the numbers we need to count are not heads of people who are coming to church, but rather heads of Christians who are actually going into the world as a result of our ministry.

God Loves The World

John 3:16 says, "For God so loved **the world...**" I find it interesting that it does not say that God so loved **the church,** or **Christians,** or **religious events,** or even **Himself,** but rather it says that He loves **The World** so much that he came to rescue us from dying after living a hopeless existence.

The Journey believes fully that if we really claim to be followers of Christ then we should follow him in his every endeavor.

Jesus gave his life for **The World.**

Should we do any less?

Change Is Upon Us

As a historian, I know all too well that civilization is going through a change.

There are certain "landmarks" that show us that civilization is evolving. Historically, changes in communication, travel, knowledge, and information indicated when a society was entering into a new era. As societies entered into new eras people began to think differently.

The world is going through those very changes now in the beginning of this 21st century. Because of these changes people outside, and, I dare say, inside, the church think and react differently to information they perceive. Therefore, it is our responsibility, as followers of Christ, to learn how to best share the information we have received from Christ just as a missionary learns how to share in a new culture. Only instead of traveling to a new culture, the new culture has come to us.

A Shocking Fact

With the exception of India and China, the United States now has the largest unbelieving population in the world. In a country so full of churches it would behoove us to ask "Why?" Maybe it is because we do not live in 1950 anymore, and our churches are still reaching out to a 1950s audience.

We also don't live in 1980, 1990, or even the year 2000. The Bible tells us that in the last days knowledge will increase and that as time goes on things will begin transpiring at a faster rate. Change is inevitable and the church needs to change with the times.

Keeping Up With The Creator

What about God? He never changes! That is true. God does not change. God's principles never change, but His methods always do.

After all, God created the world and set the whole thing into motion. The fact that we can see change around us proves that God is the author of change. *Maybe that means that if we in the church do not change our methods, than we are not following God's plan!* Therefore, for God's sake, let's continue to change. People all around us are *dying* to know Jesus.

Getting Outside Ourselves

It is time to take Jesus out of our churches, off of our shelves, out of our religious events, out of our daily devotions, and into **The World**.

Ask yourself what motivates you more... the desire of going to a religious event, or the desire of telling someone about Jesus, verbally and non-verbally. The answer may be groundbreaking.

———

The thoughts in the article may have been our goal, but in reality things would ultimately turn out differently.

In the first year of our existence, we met during the evening hours at a coffee bar downtown called The Loft. It was exciting, with all kinds of people coming. Everyone from the homeless to drug addicts came and brought their problems with them. Homeless people were actually saved, and a marriage was restored. There were even reports of suicides averted due to our ministry there.

One night I talked about reading a mystery and coming across an event or chapter that may be confusing or even upsetting. "In fact," I mentioned, "there are times when a portion of a book can upset you so much that you want to throw it away. But, don't throw a whole book away just because of one bad chapter!"

Movies are this way for many Christians as well. I have watched many movies that have a profound conclusion with a statement that would benefit and encourage many of those who watched. The only problem is that, in order to get to that point, the writers have to set the stage with a problem so that they can resolve it. Many Christians watch or hear about how the film begins and as a result focus only on the problem. They refuse to watch the movie, missing the conclusion. They preach about the problem in the movie as though that were the entire movie. As a result they miss out on an incredible ending!

As an example, consider the movie "Family Man," starring Nicholas Cage. Most Christians would naturally turn the movie off in disgust during the first scene, only to miss the journey Cage's character takes in discovering what really is important in life by the time he reaches the end of the movie!

At any rate, a homeless man came to me the next week during The Journey meeting and said, "Remember when you talked about not throwing the whole book away just because of one bad chapter? Well, I had intended on ending my life this week until I heard you say that. As I thought about my life, I realized that I shouldn't throw it all away just because of one bad spell."

Thank God! It would have been a shame if he had missed an incredible ending just because he could not stand the problem!

Overall, I feel that this first year was our best time at ministry, although it was not without its problems. We also had the "over churched" people attending. They would not commit to The Journey as their church. After all it was not on Sunday mornings, and it didn't look like a church. In Tulsa, there are people who I refer to as "church groupies." They are the ship dwellers who have fallen so in love with the ship that they cannot see the water. Every time they hear of some new exciting thing happening with a church, they come running to be a part, just in case it hits the "big-time." They simply do not want to miss out. It was very hard at times to steady the ship with all these influences abounding. But as I mentioned, The Journey's first year was productive, and some of those homeless and drug addicts now attend other churches.

As the first year came to a close, so did The Loft, and we were forced to move to another location. As a result, we ended up in a private school on the west side of the river, hidden in seclusion.

Even though we were hidden deep in the trees west of the river, we had some success there attracting college students and a full worship band, but that too soon came to an end. The band members graduated and moved on. Many of their "following" soon did as well. We had also lost the homeless, alcoholics, and drug users by relocating. It was sad that by moving from downtown to a secluded safe place we traded in those who needed Jesus for those who needed church. After meeting there for over a year and a half, several families moved to other parts of the country and we shrank to a very small group. Seeing the need to change, we left the private school and moved into homes for the next few months.

I read *The Unchurched Next Door* by Thom S. Rainer and concluded that we needed to focus on a more religious, friendly group in order to grow a stronger foundation to reach the lost. We rented a storefront and started trying to be a bit more *normal*. We changed service times to Sunday morning and actually placed chairs in rows for the first time ever! I think it was at that point that the vision for The Journey died without our realizing it.

We ended up just like any other small unsuccessful church. We had a Sunday morning service with a few Christians sitting around looking at each other, not knowing exactly why we were there. But come we did, because that is what you are *supposed* to do on Sunday mornings. As we struggled over the next two years, it became obvious to me that once again a change had to take place.

After much thought and prayer, Cindie and I decided to officially step down as pastors and *close* The Journey as we knew it. For Cindie and me, The Journey was not coming to an end, but rather simply coming to a *bend* in the road.

We simply felt that everyone's time could be better focused by placing our efforts in a slightly different direction. Cindie and I took a two-month period of much-needed rest so that we could pray and seek God for our next step. It is during this two-month hiatus that I am writing this book.

CHAPTER TEN

Oriented

In starting The Journey, I spoke to the team about task orientation vs. relationship orientation. Task orientation always seeks a new task once the first task is reached. For that reason, once you get to a point beyond which you cannot achieve the next task, this orientation collapses, and the feeling of failure sets in.

When I was a missionary in Europe as a song writer, everything was very task oriented. I was willing to do whatever it took to perform in a way that best presented the gospel to the lost. I was very single minded and, as a result, failed to build relationships with my co-workers. In fact I might have destroyed some. This type of orientation almost destroyed my own life!

When Stina turned sixteen years of age, we took her back to Europe to show her where she was born. As I came across old friends in Denmark from sixteen years earlier, I found the first words out of my mouth were apologies for who I used to be. I had said many times over the past sixteen years that I had the time of my life in Denmark but I missed it. Not that I longed for it, but that it just seemed to slip by unnoticed. Somehow it had happened, and I didn't even realize that I was having the time of my life.

I was too busy being on a mission to enjoy the incredible journey that God had bestowed upon me. I was traveling the world, performing for thousands of people, recording in one of the best studios in all of Europe. I was living the dream! But I failed to enjoy it. I was overly task oriented. As a result, sixteen years later I realized what it was I had missed. I had failed to build relationships with the very people I lived and worked with in Denmark. I didn't even know them.

Someone said that you haven't changed until you regret the way you used to be. Well now I found myself regretting who I used to be and suddenly became thankful for whom God had made me become.

There is a word in English I never fully understood until I went to Denmark and learned Danish. The word in English is "fellowship." I know you are thinking that I must be an idiot not to know the meaning of the word *fellowship*. But while in Denmark I learned that the same word in Danish is pronounced *fellowskab*. So, you may ask, what does that mean to me? Well, the interesting fact about that is the word *skab* in Danish means "closet." "Fellow-closet!" Suddenly it came home to me.

I pictured two guys locked in a closet, having to figure out how to get along before someone would let them out. Two guys on a ship, having no way to get off, must figure out how to live together! Fellow ship! To make it even more interesting, Webster's Dictionary defines the word "fellow" as "one of a pair." The Ship is God's tool to make *a pair out of individual fellows*. Fellowship!

That is what I had missed in Europe. I had managed to spend two years not developing fellowship! When I lived and worked in Denmark, I was on a ship and didn't even know who the other people were on board. I was so task oriented that, when I returned home as a missionary casualty in the midst of depression I saw it *all* as a failure. After that attempt and *failure* at ministry, I was crushed, broken, and wounded to the point of death.

Now at the close of The Journey, I look around and realize that I have developed some irreplaceable relationships. Not only do I have lifelong friends in Tulsa, but I now also have a home in the Foursquare Church denomination! Not that one denomination, or church group is more important than another, but God knew what I needed. He understood my situation. He rescued me! He has given me more than I ever dreamed of giving Him.

I remember one day while driving down the road, Stina looked at me and said, "Daddy thank God we found Foursquare! Isn't it great that we found a place where we belong?" So many years after returning from Europe, I was a misfit, not quite belonging. Now at the closing of The Journey, God had finally brought me home. Once again, I belonged.

If for no other reason than that, in the end, The Journey was a success. It brought me back into complete relationship with God and the church. Once again I was in fellowship. The members of The Journey, Foursquare members from all around the country, and my family and I are all together successfully in a relationship! Fellowship!

In my forty-five years of attending church, the Journey is the *only* church I have ever been in that did not suffer from a "church fight" at any level. I do not say that to judge other fellowships but to testify to the fact that a relationship orientation is a "God idea."

Find a relationship, and you have found God's plan. God has called us to be in relationship one with another. For God so loved the world that he demonstrated the importance of relationships by developing a relationship with us and then asked us to do the same with others for His sake.

The Journey taught me that there is no failure in ministry if it is done under God's plan. Even if you give a cup of water in the name of Jesus, God is happy. Instead of being task oriented, I learned that being relationship oriented, simply loving people no matter what, is what God desires. People are more precious than principles! Individuals are more important than institutions. Relationship is more real than religiosity. And fellowship is more fulfilling than fame.

Find a friend, and you have found God's plan for your life.

God has been much more faithful to me than I have been to Him. In the beginning, I focused on the goal that God was helping me reach. Now I have no goals, only friends and family that mean more to me than the world. My life has taken many turns, and now that I look back on it, I can see how God has been making me into the man that He loves.

In my twenties, I was a very judgmental and condemning person. I was a very "churched" person who knew the way Christians were *supposed* to act. If there was someone claiming to be a Christian who did not live up to the standards that I believed it took to be a Christian, I was the first to judge. But life has changed my perspective. I have been twice rescued.

As a result of life events, I actually became an unchurched person for a time. Having been broken because of my own selfish desires and then restored by God's love, I have become able to empathize with those who are broken. Now that I am in my forties, I love and care for people who are hurting and struggling because life has not turned out the way that they, or I, thought it should have. God has taught me how to be unchurched in my approach so that those who feel uncomfortable in church can meet the God who, in the end, will show Himself faithful.

As of the writing of this book, I have realized that the accident I suffered in 1983 has become only a chapter in my life. That is impressive to me because, up until lately, it was *the defining moment* in my life. That accident was the single event that drove me to do everything I did. I honestly thought that God took "time out of eternity" (an interesting concept if you stop and think about it) to save my life. I believed, and was motivated by the fact that, there was something *He* wanted me to do. I thought that the reason He saved me at the bottom of that cliff was so I could accomplish something great for Him!

Several months after the accident, I had to go in for a follow-up to see if my brain was working properly. As part of the check-up, I had to take a psychological test. It was full of questions that tried to trick you into saying something that proved you were crazy. I remember one question in particular that read, "Do you feel that you are here on a mission from God?"

I naturally answered, "Yes!"

I do not think that was the answer the secular psychologist was looking for, but for some reason I got away with it and was not pronounced crazy. Surely, that was another proof that God and I were in cahoots about something. It was my job to figure out what it was. As a result, I have spent most of the past 23 years trying to do that thing for which God had saved me. In a sense, I was trying to justify my existence.

I have said many times that, "God saved me for a reason. There is a reason I am alive, and I am not going to die and miss out on that reason." I have refused to let anything escape. I have not chosen my paths, but the turns I took along the way have been influenced by that event. I chose to record music for that reason. I chose to go to Europe for that reason. I chose to become a public high-school teacher for that reason. I chose to earn a Master of Arts in Theology at Oral Roberts University for that reason. And I chose to plant a post-modern church in a pre-post-modern city for that reason.

God has taken me on an incredible journey. This journey has taught me things I did not even know I needed to learn. But the one thing I have grown to learn the most was that all along I was focusing on the wrong dream. It was not my dream of doing great things for God, but rather God's dream of doing great things for me that was important.

I thought I was chasing after a dream, when, in reality, God was chasing after me with His dream. In the end, it wasn't *my* dream that I began to chase after having that accident that was motivating me. Without even realizing it, I was being motivated by God's dream of the ship. The lost people in the water drove me to do what I was doing.

I no longer have to justify my existence! God has done it for me. He really did take time out of eternity to save me. He came to earth and died on a cross so that I and billions of others could be rescued. I know that it is an old story, but it still works! Life has proven to me that God still cares! Jeremiah 29:11 says, "'I know the plans I have for you,' says the Lord, 'plans for good and not disaster, to give you a future and a hope.'"

God spoke those words to the children of Israel when they were in exile, far from the comforts of their Judean home. At that time, life was not good for them, but God still reminded them that He cared. When I look back on my life, I realize that God was trying to remind me of the same thing all the while. God's was saying, "I still care."

In the midst of all those low points, God was in the process of bringing me back home; not just to where I was before I went on the mission field, but rather back to that child-like faith where I simply trusted Him; a God who cared for me. Even in the closing of The Journey, God brought me home!

Remember that dark storm looming that I mentioned earlier? It turned out to be nothing more than a breath of fresh air. Now I am free from the bondage of needing to fulfill a mission. Free from the strains of needing to find out why I am here. Free from the religious powers that drive people to do all kinds of unnatural things. I have learned that if we will only do the natural—love people and demonstrate Christ's love to them—then God will take care of the super-natural!

When I stop and contemplate what has happened in my life, I think back to that small boy, kneeling in a back pew at church praying, "God, if you are real, show me a sign," I have to stop in amazement, as I realize, God is *still* answering my prayer!

About the Author

GENE MCMATH is an author and song writer who teaches high school history at Broken Arrow Public Schools (which includes the largest high school system in Oklahoma), while speaking and leading worship for many religious events. He travels and introduces Christians and non-Christians alike to a new way of viewing their life journey. Gene's own journey has given him insights beneficial to the human race at large.

In 1983 Gene had a life-changing experience when he accidentally drove a truck over the edge of a 300-foot cliff in the Colorado Rocky Mountains. After a miraculous recovery, he relocated to Northern Europe with his wife Cindie, where he spent two years performing and speaking in public schools, festivals, and religious events.

For over the past 20 years Gene has performed with many well-known artists and has toured extensively across the United States and throughout twenty countries on five different continents. He has written and recorded two music albums and has been a gifted worship leader in several churches.

Gene earned a Bachelor of Arts in History from Western State College of Colorado and a Master of Arts in Theology from Oral Roberts University. He is a licensed minister with The International Church of the Foursquare Gospel, with whom he founded The Journey in Tulsa.

Gene and Cindie have been married for over 25 years and have two beautiful daughters.

To download free music referred to in this book or to contact Gene for a speaking engagement, visit
http://www.GeneMcMath.com

Printed in the United States
104426LV00002B/364-399/A